Best Wishes

Bill Boyd

FAT, DUMB, AND HAPPY DOWN IN GEORGIA

FAT, DUMB, AND HAPPY DOWN IN GEORGIA

Bill Boyd

MERCER UNIVERSITY PRESS
1979 - 1999
TWENTY YEARS OF PUBLISHING EXCELLENCE

ISBN 0-86554-675-4   MUP/H502

Library of Congress Cataloging-in-Publication Data

Fat, Dumb, and Happy Down in Georgia/ by Bill Boyd

Columns republished with the permission of the *Macon Telegraph*

Boyd, Bill
     Fat, dumb, and happy down in Georgia / Bill Boyd
          pp. 6 x 9" (15 x 22 cm.)
     ISBN 0-86554-675-4 (alk. Paper).

CIP data from the Library of Congress (www.loc.gov)

Dedicated to

Harley Bowers
Don Carter
Billy Watson
Barbara Stinson

CONTENTS

FOREWORD

Bill Boyd. Fat? Yes (look at the picture on the dust cover). Happy? Obviously (check the picture again). Down in Georgia? No doubt. Dumb? If you believe *that*, I've got some beach front property in Oklahoma to sell you!

This is a book for all generations, but it is especially one for my generation. (I'm old enough to have been a combat infantryman in World War II, so I can remember the hard time of the 1930s.) While it is a book I can relate to, it is a compilation of stories and columns that Ol' Boyd has written over the years. It includes comedy, characters, heroes, and the stuff of true Southern folklore.

In his writing about his early years in Oklahoma, John Steinbeck's "The Grapes of Wrath" immediately came to mind. It is, of course, a novel about a farm family that moved from Oklahoma to California in 1939, and the hardships they endured, but how they were fiercely honest and courageous. On one occasion, Ol' Boyd lived that Dust Bowl life and learned lessons that he never forgot.

Maybe Ol' Boyd got his inclination to write from his Mama, who was his teacher in those early years. She wasn't a teacher in the formal sense of the word, but a teacher of her children as they moved from place to place, because she believed in a good education. I know that his patriotism and love of our country came from her. She had an old flag that she held while leading her children to recite the Pledge of Allegiance.

I believe he is as proud of the twenty years he spent in the Marine Corps as just about anything. You can tell it in talking to him and reading what he writes. Every ex-Marine I've ever known feels that way. That esprit de corps is not found among all veterans of the military.

I first came to know Bill Boyd in 1983 at the beginning of my first term in the U.S. House of Representatives. He came to Washington, I guess, to write a story about the new congressman from the Eighth district of Georgia. He took a picture of me and Luella (my wife) on the steps of the U.S. Capitol. That picture and the story took up most of the front page of the *Macon Telegraph*.

He invited us to come to the Over-75 Birthday Party, which occurred every year while I was in Congress, and we came. We missed only one in sixteen years. During the last one, even though I had been out of congress for several years, Luella and I were still there to cut the cake.

It was during those years that I really came to appreciate what Ol' Boyd was all about. Figuratively speaking, I sometimes thought he had a split personality. Here is this ex-Marine, fearlessly patriotic, whom I perceived as a tough, no nonsense, take-no-crap disciplinarian. And yet, most of his writing and his interests involved just plain, good folks in everyday situations, and most especially older citizens. He writes about them with warmth, humor, and respect. As you read what he writes, you come to understand he has a real soft spot for them, and you can feel it, too.

I've always believed that being at a certain place at a certain time determines the direction your future will take. I think that those of us in Middle Georgia benefitted from Bill Boyd's coming our way. While this transplanted Okie may not be able to "speak Southern" the right way, he sure knows how to "write Southern" the right way.

To my way of thinking, the only way you wouldn't enjoy and appreciate this book is if you were not able to read at all.

J. Roy Rowland

PREFACE

When I arrived in Macon in 1973, I owned several cameras and a desire to be a journalist. At that point, major newspapers—like the *Macon Telegraph*—were hiring virtually no one without a college degree. But I had a friend, Harley Bowers, for whom I had worked part-time in the late 1950s at the *Albany Herald*. He talked to a couple of people on my behalf, and Executive Editor Don Carter and Managing Editor Billy Watson trusted Harley's judgment enough to take a chance on me. Billy Watson became my mentor, and later, another editor, Barbara Stinson, molded me into something of a columnist. (She also has edited all four of my books.) Without the encouragement and assistance—and the patience—of these four people, this book probably never would have made it into print. And that's why it is gratefully dedicated to them.

ACKNOWLEDGMENTS

The publication of a book takes the efforts of many people other than the author. Here are the people to whom I shall be forever grateful in making this book a reality:

—Barbara Stinson, who edited some 2,500 columns and four books for me, including this one.

—Former Georgia Congressman J. Roy Rowland for his time and effort in writing the foreword for this book.

—Cecil Staton, Andrew Manis, and the staff at Mercer University Press for going the extra mile in producing, printing, and marketing this book.

—Nick Oza, the award-winning *Macon Telegraph* staff photographer, for the wonderful picture on the dust jacket of this book.

—Joshua David Boyd, my grandson, and Pongo, the 219-pound hound dog, for their cooperation in the making of the cover for this book. And Pongo's master, Peter Whitt for allowing us the use of his picturesque farm in Macon County.

—Former Georgia Governor Zell Miller, radio and television legend Bill Powell, and my newspaper friends, Barbara Stinson and Carol Hudler, for the kind words that appear on the dust jacket.

—Bill Weaver and Lisa Call for their help in getting numerous columns onto computer disks.

—Retired Marine Sgt. Maj. Earl Flowers for his long-ago words of wisdom that wound up becoming the title of this book.

—Last but not least, my wife, Marvalene, who did much of the hard work in getting this book together.

1

FAT, DUMB, AND HAPPY DOWN IN GEORGIA

At our duty station in Cleveland, Ohio, an old Marine sergeant major named Earl Flowers used to say, "Don't get too fat, dumb and happy here. About the time you do, you'll get orders to go to Vietnam or Okinawa or some other enchanted land."

Three years was about all a Marine could expect to stay in one place. But I put down some roots when I retired in 1973, and for more than twenty-five years I have lived in the same town. And the sergeant major will just have to excuse me this time. In Macon, Georgia, I have indeed grown fat (like a hibernating grizzly bear), dumb (like a fox) and happy (like a bullfrog under a drippy faucet on a hot summer day).

I found a comfort zone after years of moving from place to place as the son of a sharecropper and twenty years with the Marines. Stay in one place long enough to get fat, dumb, and happy? It was only a pipedream until. . . . Well, turn the page and you'll understand. . . .

Why I love my family and old folks. . . .

Why I chose to write columns when other jobs surely would have paid better. . . .

Why this pilgrim from Oklahoma became a dyed-in-the-wool Georgia boy. . . .

Why I wrote this book. . . . Fat, dumb and happy, indeed.

My Birthplace:
Is that Jenks or Jinx?

Being born in a town named Jenks is, well . . . it sounds too much like Jinx. I didn't even notice until after I left Oklahoma. Marines were always asking, "Where are you from?"

"Oklahoma," I'd say.

"Where were you born?"

"Jenks."

"Jinx?"

"No, Jenks. Spelled J-e-n-k-s."

Establishing the spelling didn't make a whit of difference. They called me "The Jinx Kid." Finally, I changed my birthplace.

"Where were you born?" someone would ask.

"Ever hear of Wedlock, Oklahoma?" I'd ask.

Of course, the answer was negative. There is no Wedlock, Oklahoma. I'd say, "Well, I was born just outside Wedlock."

Some got it; some didn't.

(My mama got it, and she didn't like it a bit. She threatened to wash my mouth out with soap, even though I was a full-grown man and on my own.)

But Marines will rag a buddy about anything. For instance, I *never* should have told anyone how many brothers and sisters I had.

"How many children in your family, Boyd?"

"Eighteen."

The whistles and hoots would begin.

"Eighteen children? Say, what did your daddy do for a living?"

I almost said, "He was a sharecropper." But I needed another answer, a retort, a comeback, something witty. If they were going to joke about it, why shouldn't I?

My attitude changed. So did my answers. "You're just like everyone else," I'd say. "Folks are always asking what a father of eighteen children did for a living, but no one ever asks what he did for a *hobby*." And sometimes I'd add, "My old man had a few crop failures, but children wasn't one of them."

A sense of humor drew laughter instead of ridicule. Pretty soon, I had an answer for just about everything. Marines liked anyone with a quick wit. (Otherwise, why would we have helped make Bob Hope so famous?) I even learned to strike first instead of reacting to barbs about my family, my hometown, and even my name. (Bill Boyd? Hey, that was Hopalong Cassidy's real name, wasn't it? Yeah, but I can't even ride a horse.)

"How did your family get eighteen children?" someone would ask.

Sometimes, I'd say, "Well, Mama was hard of hearing. When she and Daddy would go to bed at night, Daddy would say, 'Are we going to go to sleep or what?' Of course, Mama would say, 'What?' And we wound up with a lot of little 'whats' running around the house."

However, I have to be honest with you, dear reader. Daddy was married twice. He and his first wife had twelve children—Jesse, Carl, Mabel, Betty, Faye, William E. Jr., George, Russell, Neva, Clarence, Leonard and Alice—before they discovered they didn't love each other. After they split up, Daddy married my Mama and they had six "younguns"— Wilma, Curtis, William J. (that's me), Elizabeth June, Thomas, and Robert.

Daddy's children were spread out in years from 1901 to 1945. No twins, no triplets, and no help from the milkman, either. There were so many children that our parents apparently were running out of names. That's why I wound up with sisters named April, Mae, and June (all were middle names). And that's true, but I have a hard time convincing folks by the time they've heard some of these other tales.

My daddy was six weeks shy of his sixty-fifth birthday when his eighteenth child was born. I was his fifteenth, but I never complained about being so far down the pecking order. A kid born in a town that sounds like Jinx could have been the thirteenth, you know.

OK, OK, you're wondering if I told the truth about Mama being hard of hearing, right? She wasn't. She could hear a mouse walking on cotton. The truth is, we had all of those children because a train roared past our house at 4 a.m. Daddy always said it was too late to go back to sleep and too early to plow.

My Old Daddy, The Sharecropper

My daddy, the sharecropper, died when I was nine years old, but I learned a few things from him before he cashed in his chips.

First, I learned a work ethic. When I was perhaps eight or nine, my old daddy stood looking out a window at fields rendered lifeless by a harsh Oklahoma winter, and he said, "We'll be lucky if we don't starve to death this winter."

Looking back, I can see that there was little danger of that. The Reverend Providence Story and the kind folks at Calvary Baptist Church would never have allowed us to starve to death. But the old man's words had a lasting affect on me. After he died and we moved to town, I made up my mind that I'd never starve to death.

I shined shoes on the street corner, set pins at the bowling alley, caddied at the golf course. By age eleven, I was accustomed to having money in my pocket, and I was accustomed to helping out at home, too.

By the time I left for college, I was making $55 a week as sports editor of the *Okmulgee Daily Times* and $30 a weekend for running the shop for the golf pro at the country club. Think about that. In 1953, I was making $85 a week, while Daddy Philpot drove a taxi for $45 a week. I remember him saying, "I don't know about this boy even bothering with college, Maw. He's making an awful lot of money."

"You just leave him be," Mama said. "He's going to college. He's going to be the first college graduate in my family."

Well, I wasn't. Mama had to wait another forty years for a grandson (my son Joe) to become the first of her offspring to earn a college degree. But she lived to see it. And how did she feel about the fact that her son never finished college? She was very proud to have a writer in the family. She even said at one point, "Maybe Daddy Philpot was right. Maybe you didn't need to go to college."

The other lasting lesson I learned from my daddy was honesty. And Daddy Philpot reinforced that lesson—if any reinforcement was necessary.

First, you have to understand that my old daddy was as mean as a snake, but he was honest to his last dime. And I've never known anyone who worked any harder than he did to make his dimes.

He never kited a check because he never had a checking account. He didn't buy with plastic money, either. He died long before credit cards took over our lives. I doubt that he would want either one, if he were alive today. One reason I say that is because he never had a driver's license. And what can a person do with checks and credit cards without a driver's license?

But in the far corner of my mind, I can still see . . . . It happened the year I turned five years old. We were camped somewhere near Wichita Falls, Texas, and the old man was plowing fields for a landowner. Daddy was just finishing up for the day when a pudgy, red-faced man got out of a car and started an argument. He said my old man had *stolen* some money from him.

Well, sir, the old man's steely blue eyes blazed and his face flushed red with anger. He told the fat guy flat out that he'd "better take back those words and apologize for ever saying it." As they argued, the old man was gathering up the reins from a day of hard work. The reins were made of leather, at least an inch wide and very thick. About the time Daddy thought he ought to be hearing an apology, he finished gathering the reins into loops about three feet long. When the apology was not forthcoming, the old man struck.

The first lick popped like a pistol shot. The red-faced man fell backward. The old man, approaching sixty at the time, stood over him and said, "Take it back!" The man on the ground refused. Daddy hit him again and waited a moment. Still no apology. Then the real "whuppin'" began. There was no pause between licks, and it took Mama and the boys to pull Daddy off of the man on the ground. The red-faced man scrambled to his car and drove away.

A while later, the sheriff showed up and began asking questions. "He said I stole from him, and I didn't," Daddy explained. "Then I told him to apologize and he wouldn't." All of the time the old man was talking, he was looking the sheriff straight in the eye. Apparently, the sheriff believed my dad. He finally asked if the old man would swear to what he had said in a court of law. "With my dying breath," Daddy said.

I remember that the sheriff grinned and said something like, "Well, Mister Boyd, he sure shouldn't have accused *you*." Then he got in his car and drove away, and that was the last we ever heard of it.

That story was told and retold many times in my family, and I figured that if my daddy would put a licking like that on a grown man for accusing him of dishonesty, then a boy like me had better be as honest as the day is long. The older I got, the more I appreciated the lesson.

Mama
A Lady Who Knew How to Teach
(from a column published in 1979)

She didn't look like a school teacher. Her hair was never pinned up quite as neatly as a schoolmarm's. But then, schoolmarms seldom went straight from a washboard to a blackboard. She didn't have the formal education of most schoolteachers. Hers ended early in the eleventh grade. The books from which she taught weren't the latest editions. Primers were old and the covers were faded. Workbooks were tattered and sometimes pages were missing. But in a covered wagon traveling the arid roads of Oklahoma and Texas, the plump, pleasant woman found time to teach her offspring.

Her handwriting was as straight and perfect as the examples that are often posted above blackboards in classrooms. Her children tried to write as perfectly as she did, but their efforts often looked like . . . well, like notes scribbled in a moving wagon.

She was a good reader. She honed that skill by reading old Western romance magazines she borrowed from others. But her children learned from the primers, from old newspapers. Old newspapers? Maybe a writing career was spawned back then, when Adolph Hitler was mentioned more often than George Washington and Pearl Harbor seemed closer than El Paso. Her arithmetic was accurate. It had to be. She learned to figure with her grocery money—of which there never was enough. And, Lord knows, that lady could spell. She was the second-best speller in all of Ohio when she was in the eighth grade. She would look at a kid who was supposed to be in the third grade and say, "Spell 'incomprehensibility.' " If the kid hesitated, she'd say, "You'd better learn to spell it, or you'll surely suffer from it."

The woman taught her brood in the covered wagon and around campfires. When things were at their best, the youngsters could learn by the light of a kerosene lamp if the children's father was fortunate enough to find a job with a shack or old farmhouse thrown in. While her husband worked in sun-baked fields with a mule and a plow, the woman taught patience, reverence and independence right along with reading, writing and arithmetic.

And she was patriotic. She kept a flag from a long-ago parade in Tulsa, and she would hold that flag in her hand while the kids put hands over hearts and recited the Pledge of Allegiance.

For a while the family settled in west Texas, where the family lived in an adobe shack while the woman's husband worked for a rancher. The nearest school was forty miles away, so the woman kept right on teaching. Before the end of World War II the family moved back to eastern Oklahoma. The trip took months but the woman never stopped teaching. Finally, she could give thanks that her children would attend a real school full time.

How good a teacher was she? A nine-year-old boy she had taught was tested and placed in the fourth grade. He made good grades, finished high school, and even attended college for a few months. When he dropped out, it was not for academic failure.

Her lessons in reading, writing and arithmetic—and, Lord knows, spelling—eventually led her son to a writing career. Yes, in case you haven't guessed, this woman—the spelling champ, the disciplinarian, the patriotic soul with a little American flag in one hand—was my mother.

Now, would you spell incomprehensibility for me?

Daddy Philpot
The Best Stepdaddy a Boy Ever Had
(from a column first published in 1978)

The Oklahoma family scattered after the father died. The older children went to live with relatives while the young widow reorganized her life. Another man brought the family back together, a gentle man from Arkansas.

An old heap of a taxi was his only transportation. He drove it twelve to fifteen hours a day to make a poor man's dollar. But hacking wasn't much of a living in the late 1940s. He paid his way from a little black change purse with a single snap at the top. With it, the Arkansas man managed to stay close to even with the world. A driver's license was his meal ticket, like a college degree to some folks. With it, he said he could "always make a living."

When he met the young widow, she had four boys with her. The youngest was a toddler, the eldest was thirteen. Romance blossomed under a sign that flashed "Taxi Here." The Arkansas man and the widow sat on a worn bench and talked. Little boys played at their feet. Bigger boys rambled around the Oklahoma town.

A year passed before he finally popped the question. She said yes. So she scrubbed up her "young'uns" and the Arkansas man loaded his true love and her kids into his taxi and they headed for Fort Smith to get married. The couple said their vows, and whitewash was used to letter "Just Married" on the taxi for the return trip. People in the small towns smiled and waved at the newlyweds with a carload of children.

Daddy Philpot brought stability and laughter to the family. It was the best of times for the widow and her four boys. To support his ready-made family, the Arkansas man took a second job as a constable in the Oklahoma town, serving papers on people who failed to pay their bills.

Even though there never seemed to be enough money to raise those boys, Daddy Philpot doled out dimes once a week to pay for movies with Roy Rogers, Gene Autry, and the Sunset Kid. Sometimes, he'd squeeze out extra nickels for popcorn and Cokes. He did that even though Daddy Philpot always referred to movies as "foolishness."

The Arkansas man was good for the economy, always a little in debt, never hoarding money. Times were hard, but he refused to let them get desperate.

He was a country philosopher, and some of his sayings stuck with the boys he helped raise:

"Always be honest. Money can take honesty away, but it can't buy it back."

"Don't trust a talker. A man can talk just so long and keep telling the truth."

"Be careful of a man who borrows money. He's already in money trouble."

His sayings made more sense to the boys once they grew up.

Twelve years passed, and the older boys had moved away when Daddy Philpot got sick. They gathered beside his hospital bed, and their presence was like a tonic. He went home.

Another week passed, and death came to the Arkansas man. This time, the boys gathered to bury him, pooling their money for a decent funeral, a final touch of class that the Arkansas man surely would have regarded as so much extravagance.

More years passed. The widow married again and moved away. The children seldom returned to the grave in Oklahoma.

Almost twenty years after the funeral, a son checked a logbook at the cemetery to locate Daddy Philpot's grave. Beside his name was a notation: $15 due.

Yes, said the caretaker, but that is a very old debt. I pulled $15 from my pocket. Daddy Philpot was finally even with the world. It was the least I could do for the best stepdaddy a boy ever had.

Seeking the Finer Things in Life

(from a column first published in 1979)

Most of you folks don't know that Ol' Boyd once played the violin. But it's true. When I was in the seventh grade, Mama took me by the hand (which can be very embarrassing for a seventh-grader) and said, "You *will* get a taste of the arts. You will *not* grow up without some knowledge and appreciation for the finer things in life."

Already, I was discovering girls, but Mama had something else in mind when she talked about the "finer things in life." Our school was forming an orchestra for the first time, and Mama thought that would be a good place for me to start my journey to refinement.

Joining an orchestra is not much different from joining the Marine Corps, I would someday reason. You go through a line, and what you get is what you've got. I got a violin. Just like those Marine uniforms not fitting my once-skinny body, a violin didn't fit very well under my chin.

I soon discovered that the violin is not for everyone. Remember the kid who could rub his belly with one hand while patting his head with his other hand? *That* kid could play the violin. Not me. I was perhaps the most uncoordinated kid in school. To make the situation worse, I had a very stern director. He'd slap his little stick against the director's stand and hold up his hands. Everyone was supposed to be ready to play. But I was *never* ready.

Even so, Mama made sure I practiced. She made me practice until there were little grooves in my fingers from holding down the strings. And if I acted like I wanted to slack off, she'd say,

"Practice, son. Practice makes perfect." Well, practice didn't make perfect. My screeching on that confounded thing only brought cats to our house. Black cats, brown cats, white cats, calico cats, yellow cats. You see, after months of practice, my rendition of "Oh, My Darling, Clementine" was almost the exact duplicate of the feline mating call! Cats came around to see if there really was any action at our place. My good-hearted Mama fed them and kept them around because rats and mice were a problem in those days. But there were no mice at our house during my violin-playing days. However, once they found out that the noise came from my violin, most of them drifted away. Or maybe they found out I was sawing on *catgut* strings.

One big ol' tomcat turned out to be Mama's favorite, and he was the only cat allowed in the house. Mama petted him and called him "The Mop" because, anytime she spilled a little gravy, that old cat would lap it up until the linoleum was clean as a pin.

But one day Mama was trying to give some castor oil to my older brother, Curtis. As Mama wrestled with him, the bottle of castor oil slipped from her hand and spilled all over the kitchen floor. And here came the mop, going lap-lap-lap. That big dose of castor oil affected the cat about the same way it would affect you or me. The last time we saw him, he was heading across one of Daddy's plowed fields. Six other cats were a-helpin' him. Two were digging, two were covering, and two were scouting for unused ground!

Mama pined away about the old cat, and I think she might have had me playing the violin for the next four years if school officials hadn't decided to disband the orchestra. They put up a plaque to commemorate that turn of events. And I said a very fervent prayer of thanks.

Remembering Mama
(from a column published on May 30, 1993)

When she lived so far from a school that her children had to be taught at home, she made us recite the Pledge of Allegiance—with reverence in our little voices. She made sure all of us grew up to be red-white-and-blue patriots.

When my sister Wilma was wearing sack dresses and the boys were complaining about patched jeans, Mama reminded us that boy's pants *could* be made from flour sacks, too. Mama lived in wonderment that today's generation would pay good money for used jeans that she couldn't wait to throw away.

When her children could finally attend a good grammar school in Oklahoma, this sometimes rebellious son of hers didn't like for complete strangers to tell him to sit down and be quiet. A teacher whipped my hind end and sent me home. Mama whipped that hind end again and took me back to school. And I got considerably quieter.

When her sixth child (and my Daddy's eighteenth) was about to be born, she told my brother, Curtis, to keep churning that butter because she would be back in a few hours to make biscuits. She surely was disappointed at the changing times and how "that dadgummed doctor made me stay overnight."

All but one of Mama's children finished high school, and I always thought it was because she didn't want us to settle for too little in life. I can still hear her saying, "It takes *gumption* to stay in school. Anyone can quit. *Anyone*, do you hear me?"

Mama brought six healthy babies into the world. The smallest weighed nine pounds. Mama was openly critical of women who smoked and drank and didn't take proper care of themselves during pregnancy. And when she heard that a woman had a six-pound baby, she harumphed and said, "We used to throw them back when they were that small!"

When some sicko put ground-up glass in jars of baby food, I called Mama to see if anything like that happened in the old days. She harumphed again and said, "Honey, you were a breast-fed baby. Your old man would have shot anyone who messed with *that* food supply."

I lived fifty-some-odd years before I found out that Mama and her generation made cottage cheese from clabbered milk. Mama loved to talk about "the used-to-be."

Mama outlived four husbands in a row, and after the funeral for the fourth, I sat Mama down for a heart-to-heart talk. Even though she was past seventy, I knew she would marry again. "Look, Mama, I want you to stop marrying those old guys. Marry someone who will bury you." It's the only time Mama ever seemed to take my advice. She married a guy a year younger than me. I never did get around to calling him "Daddy."

Her new husband became a truck driver, and Mama, who'd never held a driver's license, traveled the country with him past her eightieth birthday. She saw sights she never dreamed she'd see. "I saw your only friend in New York," she once said. That, of course, would be the Statue of Liberty.

Sometimes, I'd get a phone call from Mama, and she'd want me to meet her at a truck stop in Atlanta. I wrote, "Isn't it something that a man my age has to go to a truck stop to see his mama?" Readers were quite amazed at Mama's adventures, and she became something of a hero, especially to women around the eighty-year mark . . . .

When fancy new rigs with kitchens, microwave ovens, and VCRs starting hitting the road, I called Mama to get a reaction. "If I wanted to have all of those things," she said, "I think I'd just stay at home all the time." She finally had to do just that. But she was sorry they decided to give up life on the road. "I kinda miss it," she said.

Mama got out of bed on the morning before her 82nd birthday to go to the bathroom. She collapsed and died almost instantly. Thankfully, Mama didn't suffer. But I still miss her sense of humor and those wonderful words of wisdom.

2

COMING TO GEORGIA: AN OKLAHOMA PILGRIM FINDS A HOME

Strange, isn't it, how our paths are guided by certain turns of events? In 1957, I was ready to leave the Marine Corps and return to college, but two things changed my mind. First, I was having a dickens of a time trying to find a worthwhile scholarship, and second, a friend was lobbying me to reenlist and help him build a golf course at the Marine base in Albany, Georgia. I finally decided to come to Georgia.

But I didn't know how to get here. When I stopped by Oklahoma to visit Mama, I asked a college graduate with a degree in geography how to get to Georgia. He gave me a most sophisticated answer: "Go to Dallas (Texas) and turn left."

Well, that got me here. But, at the time, I never dreamed that I would get fat, dumb and happy down in Georgia. And I'll tell you why. . . .

Hold the Gree-its

I've always marveled at the way Georgians talk. And I'm not just poking fun at the natives of this blessed state. Oh, all right, maybe I am poking a little fun. But where else does a single-syllable word become a two-syllable word and a two-syllable word get jammed into a single syllable?

At my first stop for food in Georgia, the waitress asked, "You want some gree-its with them aigs?" I thanked her and said that I didn't like grits. She shook her head in wonder and said, "You don't talk like a Yankee, but you must be one."

Later, when I discovered that someone had stolen the hubcaps from my 1952 Mercury, a Georgian immediately said I needed to see the "chef." Actually, the Southern contraction of "sheriff" sounds a lot like the guy in the kitchen. That's why I'm certain that a lot of Yankees—and at least one refugee from Oklahoma—have done a bit of head-shaking when they have problems and are told they need to see the "chef."

Georgians are also known to drop an "R" here and there. I remember hearing a Georgian say that a certain man "sure is impo'tant." And I'm thinking how would that person know about someone else's impotency?

Well, never worry about folks in this state dropping an "R" here and there. Just as sure as they drop an "R" from Cordele and make it "Ko-deal," they drag it down the interstate and put it on the tail-end of Alma. Yes, it's called "Almer" in South Georgia.

I heard a lawyer say he had to go to the "coat-house." Not courthouse, but "coat-house." I thought Georgia's legal eagles made so much money that they had little houses in which to hang their coats.

I certainly didn't start calling myself a Georgian right away. Shoot, I didn't even know how to blow the gnats away from my eyes at first. Soon learned, though.

More than anything else, I learned to like the people in Georgia. A pilgrim from Oklahoma can surely overlook the gnats and a misplaced "R" to be around the kind of folks I met in Albany (pronounced All-BENNY, in case you're also a pilgrim.)

After four years in Albany, the Corps moved me to Camp Lejuene, North Carolina, and then to school in San Diego. But some inner voice kept harking back to dear old Georgia. When graduation came and I was allowed to list three choices for my next duty station, I listed Albany, Doerun and Ty Ty. Got Albany again, probably because Marine Corps headquarters never had heard of the other two.

By the time I left Albany a second time, I still wasn't sure I'd come back to Georgia. But a couple of things changed my mind. After an overseas tour of duty, I was ordered to West Palm Beach, Fla., to train Marine reserves. That was great duty. The party started a few days after I arrived in West Palm Beach , and it didn't end even after I married Marvalene. We still partied.

But something was missing. There is no change of seasons in south Florida. I bought an Austin-Healey roadster and put the top down. It stayed down all winter. I told Marvalene, who was born in south Georgia and grew up in south Florida, that she really ought to experience the seasons. But she was under-whelmed. Long-handles and ear muffs didn't appeal to her.

Of course, I didn't really want to wear long-handles and ear muffs, either. But someone in Marine Corps headquarters must have been listening to that talk about the change of seasons. After another tour of duty overseas in 1969-70, my orders read: Cleveland, Ohio.

Don't know if you've ever been to Cleveland, but you've gotta love winter to love Cleveland. Did I say something about a change of seasons? Well, there ain't but two seasons up there—winter and the Fourth of July. Marvalene, who'd never seen snow until we went to Cleveland, was ready by that first January to pack up and move south. But we endured three of those awful winters before I could retire.

It was a wonderful day for the Boyds when the *Macon Telegraph* gave a 38-year-old cub reporter a chance. Yes, sir, we rolled into town in late October 1973 in a humble little Plymouth Valiant.

No one had to tell me how to get here. After two tours in Albany, I almost was a Georgian. And in wonderful Macon, there is a spring and a very long summer and an autumn and a rather short winter. Isn't it wonderful how I wound up north of the gnats and south of the snow? It won't get much better than this.

And now I am a Georgian. Period. Yes, I flunked Muley's school on how to speak Southern. No, I still don't eat gree-its, biled (boiled) peanuts, or chitlins.

Yes, I still pronounce the "r" in Cordele, as well as the one in "courthouse." But, hey, I've come a long way. When I go up North, folks say, "You sure do talk Southernlike." I say, "Yes, ma'am. Georgia adopted me. Ain't it wonderful?"

And it is. Just ask me.

Sign Here with Your "X"

(from a column published on July 19, 1996)

It isn't always easy to be a Georgian. Outsiders obviously don't regard us as highly as we regard ourselves. But that's their fault. They ought to get to know us, and then they wouldn't talk about us the way they sometimes do.

It may appear to some natives of this state that I shouldn't be speaking for Georgians. After all, I was born in Oklahoma and raised by the U.S. Marine Corps. But I have now lived in Georgia very close to half of my sixty-three years (counting my Marine days in Albany) and my claim to Georgia is by my own proclamation rather than birthright.

Regardless of what a visitor might hear, we do not hate Yankees. We like to needle folks, and if we didn't needle Yanks about being Yanks, it would be something else. On the other hand, if Georgians don't like a person, they won't needle at all. Perhaps you've heard that Georgians are clannish. If that means we tend to take care of one another, then we are guilty. But we are not clannish in a standoffish way.

We are helpful. If you have a flat tire, you won't stand beside the interstate all day or night and wonder if help will ever come. Someone will screech to a halt and offer the use of a cell phone.

We are not as backward as our image is sometimes painted by others, and I've fought some rounds about that. I'll give you an example. In the process of writing a book some years ago, I was traveling down Interstate 75 to Miami Beach. In those days, the speed limit was fifty-five miles per hour, but I drove a twenty-year-old Plymouth Fury that liked to run with its ears laid back.

I was clipping right along, doing well over the speed limit in north Florida, when I saw flashing blue lights behind me. I knew I was in trouble. But I got out of the car with a good attitude and with my driver's license and insurance card in hand. And I was grinning like a "possum eating briars." (It usually pays to approach an officer of the law in such a manner in any state.) The county mountie (deputy sheriff) who got out of the patrol car was as big as a barn door and he had a cannon on his hip. He didn't turn out to be as friendly as I was trying to be.

He eyed the Georgia tag on my car, and, right away, he started running down the state I love and the people who live there. He said he thought Georgians were under-schooled, had very little culture, and didn't have a clue about couth. Well, sir, Ol' Boyd had all he could do to keep from letting his temper get out of hand. I looked for a way to strike back, to defend my status as a resident of the great state of Georgia. But you have to be careful how you strike back at someone with a gun on his hip. Then I found a way.

When he handed me the clipboard so I could sign the speeding ticket, I struck back the only way I knew how. I put a big "X" at the bottom and handed it back to him. (For anyone who doesn't understand the "X," that's the way folks who can't write sign their names.) That fella's face turned red and then it turned purple. He lost his breath for a moment. When he could finally speak again, he turned that clipboard around and handed it back to me. With blood in his eye, he said: "OK, smart aleck, I'll give you one more chance, and this time, you'd better sign *your* name, not *mine!*"

Turns out that folks in north Florida ain't much different than Georgians, I guess. That leads me to one more conclusion. We ain't much different than anyone else, regardless of where they came from. With a little understanding, we can make anyone feel right at home.

Sign here with your "X" if you agree.

Sweet Georgia ...
What I Like About It

Someone said I ought to write about why Georgia appeals to me. It's really an endless list, but let me try:

Azaleas and dogwoods.

Country lanes and old farmhouses.

Cane-bottom chairs and front-porch rockers.

Silos and sunsets in Mennonite country.

Country churches and dinner on the grounds.

Tasseling corn and blooming cotton stalks.

Hound dogs and pickup trucks.

Wild hog suppers and the Cherry Blossom Festival.

Yard sales and flea markets

Orange leaves in fall and raindrops in spring.

The Hay House in Macon and the main street in Plains.

Zell Miller and cowboy boots.

A party of old folks . . . . or just a party.

Honest smiles and down-home preachers.

Live oaks in Savannah and Round Oak in Jones County.

Collard patches and covered bridges.

Chappell's Mill in Laurens County and the Agrirama in Tifton.

A town called Helen and a town called Helena.

Homemade walking sticks and old wheelbarrows.

Hearing someone say, "Y'all."

Hearing someone say, "Amen."

Mailboxes with flowers painted on them.

Peach orchards in the spring.

Uncle Remus Museum in Eatonton.

Stone Mountain and St. Simons Island.
The town square in Forsyth.
Square dances and square people.
Pole beans and turnip greens.
Spanish moss and Mossy Creek Barnyard Festival.
Carolyn Crayton dressed up as Dolly Parton.
Roads leaving Atlanta.
Cows with egrets on their backs.
Raw peanuts and roasted peanuts.
Overalls and pocketknives.
Slow-flowing rivers and slow-talking country folks.
Pecan trees and pecan pie.
Country music radio stations and Laura Starling.
Killer rabbits and friendly faces.
The Masters Tournament and Fred Couples' golf swing.
Farm barns and auction barns.
Watermelon patches.
Swampland Opera and dirt basketball courts.
A grand day with a grandkid.

Well, that ain't all, but I've run smack-dab out of room on this subject.

3

FAMILY MATTERS:
THE HAND THAT HOLDS THE
CLICKER RULES THE ROOST

At our house, my hand nearly always holds the clicker. Marvalene hands me the remote control. I think she likes to feed my fragile male ego. My kids found a way to get their own TV sets—just so they could have their own clickers, I'm sure. But Josh, the grand-kid, loves a battle. He won't give up the clicker no matter what. He'll hide the clicker whenever he hears my footsteps crossing the kitchen floor toward the den. "Where's the clicker?" I'll ask. The sly little rascal will say, "I'll help you look for it." If I started digging through the cushions where he stuffed it, he'll say, "You're cold, Grandpa, real cold." Of course, I knew I was red hot and about to take control of the roost again. Turn the page and read about the people who share my roost. They are a curious collection, I know, but they are the people who truly love me. . . .

Old Papers . . .
And, Oh, the Memories
(from a column published on May 13, 1991)

Digging through some old papers the other day, Marvalene came across a certificate that really jogged our memories. It was a guarantee on a set of rings. Twenty-five years ago at this time, I was in-between rings with a five-foot, blond-haired lady in South Florida. I was crazy about her, but a recently failed marriage made me go slow. Let me tell you how we wound up with that certificate.

I showed up in West Palm Beach in late 1965 to train Marine reservists. I was single and, because I'd just spent thirteen months in the Far East, I longed for the company of those wonderful American women. In a place like the Palm Beaches, a young bachelor can die from overindulgence in such a pastime.

I met Marvalene just in time. We went kinda steady, broke up for a while, and then started going real steady. But marriage? No way, José.

Still, I missed the heck out of her when I went to the Naval Hospital in Jacksonville to undergo hearing tests and wound up staying a whole month before they finally installed my first hearing aid. Fact is, I missed her so much that I bought a ring to take home to her. It wasn't an engagement ring, but a pearl ring. I called it a "friendship" ring.

"Don't get any ideas," I told her. "I don't even want to *think* about marriage."

"Me, either," Marvalene said.

Both of us were lying through our teeth.

But then I did something I never thought I'd ever, ever do. No, I didn't propose. I put extensions on the foot pedals in my Austin-Healey roadster so a five-foot lady with a pearl ring could drive it. Now I ask you, was that pure mush or what?

A couple of months later, I went to summer camp with the reservists for a lonely two weeks. I thought about where I'd been and where I was going. I was hitting on thirty-one, didn't have a child in this world, and was played out with the playboy's life. When I got back to West Palm Beach, I told Marvalene how much I'd missed her and she said she'd missed me, too. She also said that she'd taken real good care of the Healey. I should have seen true love shining through right then.

But even when the time came, Ol' Boyd didn't propose in the traditional manner. No bended knee, no little ring box in hand. One evening I mumbled something like, "You know, maybe we ought to just, uh, you know. . . ."

"We ought to what?"

Honest to goodness, my Marine voice *squeaked* when I said, "Get married?"

I really did say it as a question.

"Maybe so," said my bride-to-be.

"Well, I don't have a ring."

"This one is fine," she said, holding up the hand with the pearl.

"Naw, we can do better."

So I took Marvalene shopping—at Sears. It had a wonderful diamond counter, and we picked out a three-ring set, an engagement ring and matching wedding bands. The cost was $257.50, and the set came with a written guarantee. That's what Marvalene found the other day in the old papers.

We got married on September 10, 1966, in Green Acres (yes, that's really the name of it) Baptist Church, and we took off on a two-week honeymoon in the Healey.

We spent some time the other day reminiscing about that trip—how it rained everywhere we went and how she had to stick tissues along the convertible top to keep water from dripping into her lap.

We talked about other cars—a Mustang Sprint, a Cougar, several Cadillacs, an old Plymouth. We also talked about kids—two who have lived with us and several more who weren't really our own but seemed like it.

Then I pointed to the guarantee.

"Did you know your rings came with Sears' money-back guarantee?"

"Sure did."

"Ever think about asking for a refund?"

"A time or two."

My heart stopped beating.

"Really? When?"

Marvalene laughed and it was a happy laugh. "I'm just kidding."

"Thank goodness. Will you do me a favor?"

"Sure. What is it?"

"Quit digging in those old papers. My heart can't stand it."

Joe
The Adopted Kid Who Raised me
(gathered from several columns)

Every time January 26 rolls around, Joe gets presents like it's Christmas or his birthday, and his parents sit around and talk about January 26ths that have passed. You see, that's Joe's special day, the day he moved in with us.

Marvalene and I had been married a little more than six years in early 1973. We'd been a footloose and free-spirited pair. We'd had a lot of fun. We'd traveled the country from sea to shining sea. We'd danced under the moonlight and we'd dined in some pretty romantic restaurants. We'd done everything we'd wanted to do . . . except have a baby. Oh, we'd tried nature's way of making babies, and even though we were reasonably sure we were doing the right thing, we'd had no success.

Rather than try to find out whose "fault" it was that things weren't working out, we decided in 1972 to try the adoption route in Cleveland, Ohio, where the Marine Corps held us captive through two awful winters. (Let's face it, if a couple spends two winters in Cleveland and doesn't make a baby, it's time to try adoption.) On the day after Christmas, a caseworker told us that we'd have a new addition very soon.

On January 22, 1973—a snowy Monday in Ohio—the caseworker brought a little guy to see us. He was just twenty months old. He looked around, played with some of the toys we had accumulated for the big event, then left with the caseworker after a couple of hours. Two days later, he visited us again. He stayed all day and, when the caseworker tried to take him away, he put his arms around my neck, hung on tight, and screamed bloody murder. On Friday, the kid moved in—lock, stock and barrel. Actually, he came with the clothes on his back and the bottle in his hand. The Welfare Department felt confident we'd furnish everything else.

We had already picked out the name Timothy Joseph and decided to call him Joe. We got down on the floor that January 26 and played until his new daddy fell asleep right there on the carpet. We played all weekend. There wasn't—and still isn't, I'm sure—a whole lot of things to do in Cleveland in January. By the time he'd been with us a year, we were ready for a big celebration. And we celebrated that January 26 in Macon. We celebrated a lot of others here, too. And we always tried to make that day special for him.

On one January 26, we finished up a playhouse. On another, we installed a gym set in the backyard. His mama usually cooked her specialty on that day—home-made tacos. Since that tradition goes back farther than Rio Bravo and Del Taco, it was a special treat in his childhood.

We never made it a secret that he was adopted. We called him "the catalog kid," and we told him why: "Other parents go to the hospital and whatever is placed in their arms is what they've got to take home with them. But we picked you out of a catalog. You are a special kid." That gave him a ready comeback any time his schoolmates teased him about being adopted.

Joe got a good education and earned a degree at Mercer University. As this book goes to press, he's a teacher at Houston County High. He also brought me a grandson, Joshua, the subject of another part of this chapter.

Twenty-five of those "special days" have passed, and Joe is now a partner with Marvalene and me in an antiques and collectibles business that we established in 1995.

But even when an adopted kid grows up, his special day is still very special. And, yes, having him around is certainly worth giving up the nightlife and the moonlight dancing. Just ask Marvalene, the dancer supreme, and Ol' Boyd, the wallflower.

Do we ever suffer lapses of insecurity because we aren't his birth parents? No. We were there when he was running a temperature and when he was running the bases at the ballfield. We held his hand when he had a tonsillectomy and we held a party when he graduated from college.

Simply put, we *are* his parents. And nothing can change that.

Wonderful Wanda
Making a Commitment to God
(from a column published on March 10, 1996)

Wonderful Wanda has found her niche. I'm sure of it, and I'll tell you why. But first, let me recap this young lady's first twenty-two years and eight months on this earth.

You may recall that Wanda moved in with the Boyds when she was fifteen. (We never officially adopted her so her last name has remained Greenauer.) And her presence changed my life. For one thing, I had to learn to wear more clothing around the house. Wanda also softened me up a little. I was used to disciplining son Joe, and I didn't mind using some Marine language to do it. When I railed at Wanda, she cried. (How does an old Marine deal with that?)

But she has been a joy, watching her catch up on her education (she was two years behind in school when she moved in with us.) She also attended college for a while. Then, she began working as a paraprofessional at Morgan Elementary School and she started paying her own way. Until then, Marvalene and I had furnished her a car. As she became more independent, she wanted to buy her own. She wanted to pay for her own car insurance. She even lugged a bag of groceries into the house now and then.

Most parents would rejoice at such a turn of events. I decided that I'd rather pay for her car than see her grow up so quickly.

But the biggest change started after she went to visit our longtime Mennonite friends, Lloyd and Viola Swartzentruber, in Macon County. In their church, Wanda made a commitment to God. At the time, she said she had no intention of joining the

Mennonite church. She even told Lloyd and Viola that. But she began to take up their ways. She quit cutting her hair. She started to wear dresses instead of the ever-present jeans and T-shirts. She stopped repeating some of the Marine phrases that she had learned from me. Wanda gave up television, got rid of hundreds of country music CDs, and took down the movie posters in her room. She became a kinder, gentler person. Indeed, she became a more-wonderful-than-ever Wanda.

For her twenty-second birthday last July, Wanda asked for Mennonite-style dresses. Marvalene had some made. The next day, she put the Mennonite covering on her head. Not long after that, she told us that she was going to join the Mennonite Church.

The more time Wanda spent in Macon County, the more she realized that she wanted to live in the Mennonite community and be close to the church and the people. Becoming a Mennonite, however, is no easy task for someone not raised in the Mennonite church. It requires commitment and study. She had to learn eighteen "articles of faith" in training sessions with the bishop of the church before she could be baptized. It was a soul-searching time and a learning experience for my girl. But she made one thing quite clear: "This (her conversion) isn't about being a Mennonite," she said. "It's about being a Christian. It's about a commitment to God."

Wonderful Wanda was baptized and became a full-fledged member of the church. And many doors will open for her. She was telling me one recent night that she wants "to do missionary work so much that it makes my mouth dry." Come summertime, I expect that she will be leaving for some faraway place to do just that. I just hope it's not so far that I can't visit now and then. And when she returns, she will probably live in Macon

County, get married, and have a big family. Having a big family is also a Mennonite tradition, you know.

So Wanda has indeed found her niche. She is very happy. And her happiness has counted heavily with Marvalene and me over the past seven years.

(As this book goes to press, Wonderful Wanda is looking for another mission. She spent a year at a children's home in Virginia, and then taught at the Mennonite School in Macon County for two years. She is very happy with who she is and the lifestyle she has chosen.)

Joshua David Boyd
He's a Keeper
(from a column published on January 17, 1992)

By now, you may have heard that Ol' Boyd has a grandchild. I haven't said a whole lot about Joshua David Boyd's arrival because I didn't get to spend much time around him. He shipped out with the Marines (or at least one Marine—his daddy, Joe) to California. But people have asked plenty of questions about Josh, and the question most often is "How much did he weigh?" Do people ask that because they can't think of anything else to say or do they really want to know how much a baby weighed? Well, okay, I'll tell you. Josh was a heavyweight. He tipped the scales at eight pounds, fifteen ounces. People whistle and make awe-inspired remarks when they hear that.

Marvalene and I don't know much about birth weights. We have one adopted son, one foster daughter, and several other kids who've belonged to us to one degree or another. So I called an expert—my mama in Arkansas. She brought six of my daddy's 18 children into the world. I figured she'd have some observations on the subject. "Mama, did people make a big fuss over babies' weights when you were having babies?"

"No, but mothers remembered."

"Remembered? For how long?"

"Well, I don't know. I ain't through living yet."

"You mean you . . ."

"Still remember? Sure, I still remember. Say, how much did your grandbaby weigh?"

"Eight pounds, fifteen ounces."

"He was a runt, wasn't he?"

"A runt? Everyone out here thought he was King Kong. Why, another woman at the same hospital had one that weighed just a tad over 6 pounds."

"Really? Shoot, we used to throw 'em back when they were that small."

"You . . . .what . . . ."

"Just kidding, son, just kidding."

"Well, who was the smallest of your six?"

"Wilma, the first one."

"And how much did she weigh?"

"Exactly nine pounds."

"And she was the *smallest*?"

"Sure was."

"And what about me?"

"Well, let's see, Curtis came next. He weighed 11 pounds and an ounce."

"And then me, right?"

"Yes, you weighed eleven and a half pounds. You were a big'un."

"Was I the biggest of them all?"

"No, June was the biggest. She was exactly twelve pounds. Then I started having small babies again."

"Tommy and Bobby?"

"Yes, Tommy came in at nine and a half pounds and Bobby weighed ten pounds and seven ounces."

"And then, how did we gain weight? Joe says Josh is eating him out of house and home, and he gained three pounds in a couple of months. Serves him right, though. He tried to eat me out of house and home for eighteen years."

"Well, you started liking table food right away. I used to dab gravy on my finger and you'd just smack your lips like crazy when you ate it."

"Maybe that's why I hate gravy today."

"You hate gravy? You *grew up* on biscuits and gravy. What's got into you lately?"

"Well, I don't like. . . . Hey, don't get me off the subject. What was the average weight of a baby back in the old days?"

"Somewhere between nine and ten pounds, I suppose."

"Well, why are babies so much smaller today?"

"Women eat and drink and smoke too much when they're pregnant. At least, that's what I think. Plus they sit around a lot and get too fat."

"But you didn't."

"You *know* I didn't sit around. Why, I was churning butter when it was time to have Bobby. I told Curtis, 'You keep churning. I'll be home before nightfall and I want this fresh butter for some biscuits I'm going to bake'."

"And did you get home by dark?"

"No, that dadgummed doctor said I had to stay overnight."

"Well, you had a big baby."

"Not *that* big. He weighed just ten pounds, seven ounces."

"So why didn't you throw him back, Mama?"

"Oh, I thought he was big enough to keep."

Nudie bathing
Coping with the Flood of '94

The inconveniences of the Flood of '94 pressed us to the limit, didn't they? Well, you don't know the half of it until you've heard about my Saturday night bath. Actually, it was a Saturday night shower, but it's quite a tale nonetheless. Now let me explain that I can't start my day without a shower. I prefer a *hot* shower. If the water heater is on the blink, then a cold shower will do. But I must have my morning shower.

When the flood came, our water supply turned to a mere dribble by Thursday morning. Oh, I still got my shower. Even a little hot water made it to the shower head and, although it took longer than usual, I didn't feel like I'd missed a shower.

On Friday morning, the water supply was less than a dribble, and by Saturday morning, I had to take what my mama used to call "a sponge bath." I felt dirty all day. By then, Wanda couldn't stand it any longer, and she rounded up towels and such, and she set out to Uncle Buddie's house. He has his own well and doesn't have to depend on a water plant built in a swamp.

I made it through the day on the sponge bath and, by 9 p.m., I was playing solitaire on my computer to take my mind off the feeling of grunginess. That's when the gully-washer came. It was raining by the bucketful.

My dear wife stuck her head in the computer room and said, "Why don't you get out in the back yard and wash off?"

"Huh?"

"Wanda is in the front yard washing her hair. You can go out in the back yard. . . ."

It sounded like a wonderful idea. "But I can't take a bath with clothes on," I said.

"So? Take them off."

"And go out there buck naked?"

"It's dark," Marvalene said.

Was this the conservative, countrified, reserved woman I married twenty-seven years ago? Well, what the heck. Naked as a jaybird, I streaked out the back door with a bottle of shampoo in one hand and a bar of soap in the other. Across the patio I went and into. . . . Good grief, it was the coldest water I'd had on my bod since. . . . I couldn't remember a colder shower. I was hopping around and (without my hearing aids) yelling about how cold it was. As I started washing my hair, I realized that I had company—Marvalene. Both of us were squealing.

Wanda, still in the front yard, heard all of the noise, she later said, and worried what the neighbors might think. "Over here!" Marvalene said, motioning me to the edge of the roof. Folks, say what you want, the eave of a house makes a pretty good shower in the midst of a rain storm.

About five minutes was all I could stand out there. Then I streaked back through the house and soon made myself presentable. I poked my head out the front door and laughed at Wanda standing out there in the rain with her hair all tweaky clean. But she glared at me and said, "You made enough noise to wake the dead. I'll bet the neighbors saw you!"

"It's okay. I feel *so* good."

In ensuing conversations, Marvalene and Wanda wound up with a bet. Wanda thinks Marvalene and I were the only shower-desperate people who washed up—buck naked, mind you—in their backyard during this water shortage. A steak dinner is at stake.

Now tell me, dear reader, did the Flood of '94 make you do something wild and crazy, too?

Bypass Surgery
Two Extra Belly Buttons and an Appetite
(from a column published on January 10, 1993)

What is that classic opening for a horror story? "It happened one dark and stormy night. . . ." My horror story began on a bright and sunny December 15 when the doctor said, "Bypass."

I'd been feeling lower than whale droppings for months, so I called an old friend, Dr. Ellis Evans. He said I should talk to Dr. Alan Justice, an internist. Shortly afterward, I was tramping on a treadmill. The heart monitor went wacko.

Dr. Justice put a nitroglycerine tablet under my tongue and told me to lie down while he went looking for a cardiologist. An hour later, I was checking into the Medical Center of Central Georgia.

The Med Center? Good grief, hadn't we just printed a story critical of the Med Center's new $30,000 Christmas tree? I decided to tell them that I thought the tree was lovely and I'd be glad to pay for it while I was there. (And I think I did.)

I won't bore you with all of the details of bypass surgery. So many people have gone before me that it's now as common as a hangnail operation. Or, at least, that's what people said to placate this old man.

Well, I didn't have any problems with heart specialists. They were the first doctors I've met who didn't come into the room putting on a rubber glove and telling me to roll onto my side. These doctors were checking something besides the prostate. And they found something that made them move quickly.

Dr. Chuck Hawkins told me on Monday afternoon that I would get a heart catheterization on Tuesday afternoon. I watched on a television screen as they pumped dye into my main arteries and a reasonably bright second-grader could have pointed out my blockages.

Back in my room, Dr. I. J. Shaker uttered that dreaded word: Bypass. In fact, he said, he'd make it a double. When? "This afternoon," he said.

A few minutes later, two guys—who probably got their training by shearing sheep somewhere in Montana—showed up with electric razors and shaved everything except the top of my head and the top of my toes. I had to giggle when they mowed under my arms, but that was my last laugh for a while.

Waking up in intensive care has to be the low point of my fifty-seven years. I could only lie there and tell myself that I'd get better by the hour. Marvalene and morphine helped me believe that.

One of the more interesting adventures in bypass surgery comes when medical folks start disconnecting everything they hooked up during the operation—tubes, wires, and needles. When a burly fellow pulled those two drainage tubes out of my chest, I'm sure the sheep in Montana heard me squall.

In a mere forty-eight hours, I was in a private room. But I was starving to death. I hollered for food. Someone set a bowl of watered-down grits in front of me. I told them to bring me some *real* food. I got Jell-O.

By the time the hospital staff decided that I was ready for some real food, fruit baskets from my readers began arriving. Ol' Boyd was the happiest monkey in Macon, Georgia. I ate every banana they sent. And when the bananas were gone, I ate pears.

You sent hundreds of cards, too, dear reader. Hundreds. It was very uplifting. Thank you.

In a couple of days, I was feeling so well that I decided to take inventory and see what was new about the old bod. Of course, I noticed the foot-long incision that makes me a life member of the "zipper club." Then I also made a rather startling discovery. Veins obviously are meant to carry blood in just one direction. Well, the doctors got my bypasses in backward. Now, anytime I get embarrassed, my *feet* get red.

Dr. Evans, who visited me frequently, said he made his own startling discovery. "I was in the operating room when they opened your chest and laid your heart out in the open. And do you know what's printed on the underside of it? 'Surplus property of the U.S. Army.' Now we know where Marines get their hearts."

My inspection also revealed that I now have three belly buttons—one that I've had for fifty-seven years and two that were left where the drainage tubes had been inserted into my chest. So what, you ask? Well, I don't want to be a beach freak, so I've arranged for a tattoo artist to disguise them as an extra set of eyes. I've already taught the left one to wink.

Another thing I learned was that a writer has to be very careful what he puts in print. For instance, I merely *suggested* that bypass surgery *might* be good for one's love life. And what happened? Some middle-aged women were trying to check their husbands into the Med Center, pleading all the way, "Oh, c'mon, honey. I know your heart is okay, but try the operation. You know that Bill Boyd said. . . ."

Before I put this subject to rest, let me make three points:

- The Med Center is every bit as good a medical facility as I'd heard it was, and plenty good enough that I'm not going to gripe about the price of its Christmas tree.

- The nurses there are the very best. There never will be enough Frances Sewells, Geraldine O'Neals, and

Tammy Booths. But they'll just have to forgive me for saying that the best nurse of all was Marvelous Marvalene, my home companion.

- If I ever have to do this again, I'd like to have the same hospital, the same doctors, the same nurses, the same dedicated family members at my side, and the same wonderful people out there in reader-land pulling for Ol' Boyd.

But if that should happen, I have no idea how I would disguise two more belly buttons. . . .

An Empty Nest

I think Marvalene and I finally have an empty nest. You know that some parents have a hard time dealing with the sudden absence when their young move out. But we've had enough move-outs that. . . . Well, let me back up.

Marvalene and I were married for six years without any children, and we didn't complain . . . until we noticed that just about all of our relatives and friends had children. Oh, we tried to have children. Yes, sir, we may have been a little countrified, but no one had to explain the basics of conception to us.

So we decided to try an alternate route. On January 26, 1973, a little guy twenty months old adopted us. and we have seldom had any time alone since then. Marvalene kept Joe constantly at her side for the next four or five years. I think Joe had started first grade before he spent a night away from home. Joe obviously liked being at home. Even as he grew older, we had to coax him to spend the night with a friend down the street. It's the only way his parents could have a romantic evening alone.

Our first brush with the empty-nest syndrome happened when Joe got his driver's license. Poof! He was gone. So we tried having a romantic evening alone. Poof! He would magically reappear.

Just when Joe was entering Mercer University and learning how much fun it was to stay overnight at the frat house once in a while, a wonderful thing happened in our lives. The young lady I call Wonderful Wanda moved in with us. Now that was an experience. A girl in my house? I had to clean up my language and even wear pajamas. Good grief.

After living in a children's home for six years, Wanda was in hog heaven at the Boyd house. And she stayed right there, too.

"Wanda, why don't you get yourself a date," I'd say.

Marvalene would frown and say, "She'll get a date when she's good and ready. And not before!"

Wanda would snuggle up to Marvalene and give me a look that said to buzz off.

Joe got married, had a son, went through a divorce . . . and moved back in with us while he finished college. Then he was gone again.

But Wanda was always there . . . until the summer of 1996. That's when she decided to do some missionary work at a children's home in Virginia.

But, just as she was moving out, Joe was moving back in. By then, Joe was a school teacher but he needed to finish courses for his certification and work on a master's degree. And since his son, Josh, was living with him, we asked him to move in with us so we could help look after the grandkid. Joe commuted to his teaching job at Houston County High during the day and worked on his master's degree at night. That was a year and a half ago. And all the time, Joe was grumbling that "I shouldn't be living with my parents at my age."

Recently, Joe bought a new house. He and Josh were more than ready to move, and they did. Miss Marvalene and I finally had a night alone in our house, too. But it wasn't very romantic. My back was aching from all of the moving. On Thursday morning, I stood looking at two empty bedrooms. Wanda won't be back. She's living in Macon County these days, and she, too, is teaching school.

Do we finally have an empty nest? Looks good. I didn't have to shout my way into a bathroom. I didn't have to ask Josh if he used the wrong toothbrush again. I said, "My lady, I think we indeed have an empty nest."

"Well, I don't know," she said, "Josh says he's coming back for the weekend."

Just my luck, too. By the weekend, I figure my aching back ought to be okay, so I was thinking about a candlelight dinner, soft music in the background. . . . But, what the heck. Who needs an empty nest anyhow?

4

On the Road

When Billy Watson, managing editor of the Macon Telegraph, told me to hit the road in January of 1974, he wasn't firing me. He wanted stories from the outback of Georgia—the small towns, the country stores, the farm fields, the quaint churches, the old grist mills, even the deserted and decaying railroad stations. Along the way, I had a few personal adventures. This was life on the road. I had fun. I was well on my way to being fat, dumb, and happy down in Georgia, and I didn't even know it at the time.

A Striking Tale
(from a column published on June 16, 1993)

Somewhere between Hawkinsville and Abbeville, I met my first snake of the season. It happened because I saw a country scene that needed photographing, and I pulled to the shoulder of the road.

Of course, I'm always careful where I step. I've met snakes before. But because I'm cautious, none has ever bitten me. I was careful as I left the roadway, camera in hand, venturing through grass and weeds to a field of stubble and golden bales of straw. My, what a picture it made.

I also was careful as I returned to the car and put the camera back in the trunk. Then, as I started to close the trunk on my car, I saw it. In retrospect, I think it might have been a black snake. Yes, I know they are friends of our environment. They eat rodents and ugly creatures like that. At that moment, however, I didn't take the time to check out the make of the snake that was boldly crossing the highway, *directly at my car*.

Cold chills ran up my spine and every hair on the back of my neck had a little mountain (a goose bump, that is) on which to stand. Naturally, I looked for a means of escape. So I stepped onto the flat surface behind the license plate with my right foot and put my other foot inside the trunk. I figured that the snake was taking the shortest distance between two points and that it would emerge from the other side of my car and be gone.

I leaned toward the right side of the car and watched. No snake. I waited longer. No snake. Hmmmm. Snakes like shade on a hot day. Had this monster decided to camp out under my car? Surely, the heat from the engine and the exhaust system would make it unbearable. So I waited and watched. Still no snake.

Could it have made a ninety-degree turn along the shoulder? That seemed unlikely. I thought about bending down and poking my head under the trunk and trying to look beneath my car, but I had a vision of the snake turning out to be a vicious, human-hating rattlesnake that would strike me directly between the eyes. I tried thumping on the side of the car. No snake. Well, what to do, what to do . . . .

A pickup truck approached from the north. It stopped and I tried to swivel my body enough to talk to the driver. I heard a chuckle and a male voice saying, "You look kind of up in the air this morning."

"This isn't funny. There's a snake under my car. Would you take a look and let me know where it is?"

The man leaned over a little and looked down. He shook his head. "Don't see no snake," he said.

"How about *getting out* and looking around?" I asked.

"Now don't let some little ol' snake get your goat, mister."

"This ain't a little ol' snake."

He laughed again, put his truck in gear, and drove away.

Well, I certainly wasn't going to stand in the trunk of my car all day. So I made a few calculations. Let's see, a snake can strike half the length of its body, right? So, even if that sucker was ten feet long—and it had certainly looked that long coming across the road—it couldn't strike but five feet.

Hah! I could jump five feet. Or could I? At my age and weight. . . . It was a mighty jump, and I hit the roadway with all of the grace of a dropped sack of cement. But I was *free*! Or was I?

I whirled around. No striking reptile. Thank you, Lord. I peeked under the car. No snake there, either. But was it hiding behind one of the tires just waiting for me to step close enough?

At a safe distance, I looked under the car from a different angle. No snake. Where had it gone? Boldly, I reached and opened the car door, and, bracing one hand on top of the car and one on top of the door, I took a five-foot lunge into the car. I cranked the engine and pulled away. No snake. I had an awful thought. Was it wrapped up in the steering? I gave the wheel a couple of yanks. Well, I'd just have to put that critter out of my mind. . . .

On the other hand, maybe I should run the car through a car wash just in case. And what would car-wash employees do if a ten-foot snake came slithering out?

Where was that snake anyhow?

Shiver-shiver.

The "Silver Bullet"
(from a column published on August 10, 1992)

I'm getting old. I sat down the other day and tried to make a list of every car I've ever owned. I couldn't do it. Well, there is one car I will never forget—a 1985 Olds that still sits in my driveway.

If you and I have met in the past few years, you probably met my car, too. I named it "The Silver Bullet." It didn't get the name from its color. It looks a lot like the silver beer can seen on TV commercials, except with the front squished down to a wedge. That name was the only irreverent thing I ever said about the car.

We bought it in the spring of 1987. We were looking around the used car lot at Riverside Ford when my wife spotted the Olds. "Oh, I love that car," she said. A salesman said it was a trade-in and that it hadn't been checked out by the mechanics yet. We looked around, but Marvalene kept pointing back at the Olds. Finally, I started dickering for the Olds, and in about nothing flat, Marvalene owned it. The title was put in her name, and it was really supposed to be her car. I certainly didn't need it. I had Big Red, the Lincoln.

Just when Marvalene was getting settled into the Olds, gas prices took an awful jump, and she made the mistake of bragging about the gas mileage she was getting in the Olds. Within a few days, she was trying to figure out how to park a football field on wheels, and I was heading out of town in *her* Olds.

It turned out to be a very dependable little beer can, uh, car. Besides, Marvalene was right about the gas mileage. It would get thirty around town, thirty-five on the road. It soon became *the* transportation at the Boyd house. It made two trips to California, half a dozen to Florida, several to Oklahoma, at least one to Ohio.

It did so well over the years that, lately, when anyone started bragging about the durability of some foreign car, I loved to tell them about my American-made Olds. Sure, I once said the engine was Japanese-made, and I called the car an Oldsmobishi. But, honest, it was just a joke.

The folks at Palmer Tire got to know the Olds. They put several sets of tires on it and rotated them regularly for five years. And usually, one of them would ask, "Don't you think it's time we aligned that front end?" I'd say, "Well, run your hand over those front tires and tell if you think we need to." It never seemed to need alignment. So I'd say, "Well, if it ain't broke, let's don't fix it."

One guy at Palmer Tire used to mimic the TV commercial where an old guy leaving a shop in his dependable car would say, "See you again, boys."

Eventually, the guys at Palmer Tire, my mechanic, Jimmy Cunningham, and even my irreverent kids stood in awe of the Olds. As the car approached the 200,000-mile mark, I told everyone who would listen that not only had the engine never needed any major repairs and didn't burn any oil, but that the front end *still* hadn't been aligned.

Recently, I told Marvalene that there was no need to think about trading it. No one wanted a car with so many miles on it. But Wanda, then in college, spoke up. "I want the Olds."

"Huh?"

She said it again. And again.

I kept saying, "You're nuts."

She finally convinced me last weekend.

"Look," she said, "it's got more pep than anything else in the driveway, it's got a *wonderful* stereo, and it gets great mileage. I want it."

"OK," I said. "You can have it, but I've got something to do first. C'mon, let's take a ride."

We drove a few miles down the interstate. "Look at the odometer," I said.

She leaned over, and we watched it turn to 200,000 miles.

"Now you can have it."

Well, sir, she cleaned and polished that car until you could eat off the hood. I walked outside one Sunday morning and stood admiring the Olds. It's a nice-looking car. For a moment, I even wanted it back. But I've got a newer car. It's kinda reddish purple. And it needs a name. . . .

The Price of Air

Right away, I knew the lady behind the counter at the convenience store was not going to like the conversation. Maybe she'd heard my opening line before. "It's gonna cost a quarter to get a little air in my tire?" I asked with all of the indignation I could muster.

Her shoulders drooped in resignation. "Yes." She didn't even say "sir." But asking for free air these days makes me a beggar, and no one says "sir" to a beggar.

"When did this start?" I asked.

"A couple of months ago," she said.

"And whose idea is it?"

"Well, I suppose you could blame several people."

"All right, name them and I'll have a talk with them."

For the first time, she smiled and I saw a cat hovering over a cornered mouse.

"Start with yourself."

"Me? I never wanted to pay for air."

"But you like the price of gas at convenience stores?"

"Aw, c'mon, lady."

"Air is still free at full-service stations, I understand."

She had me there. I really am one of those cost-conscious Americans who prefers to do the pumping and save. But I didn't want it to come to paying for air. Surely, someone else was to blame for this.

"Who else is to blame? Just tell me, who else?"

"That city councilman of yours."

"Who?"

"You know. Old what's-his-face, the one who wanted an ordinance requiring air hoses at self-service gas stations."

"Ed DeFore?"

"Yes, that's the name."

"But that ordinance never passed."

"Well, let's just say that the man who owns this store saw the handwriting on the wall."

"The owner, huh?"

"Yes, he's the other one who gets the blame, I guess."

"OK, get him out here, and let's straighten this thing out."

"Can't do that. He lives in Columbus."

"Good grief. We're back to that."

Why is it that every time I want to talk to the owner of a convenience store, he or she lives in Columbus or Shreveport or Miami?

Well, I'd made my list, and at least three people needed a good talking-to: Ol' Boyd, Ed DeFore and the owner of a convenience store. Meanwhile, the lady behind the counter was gazing steadily at me.

Noticing that she wasn't all that young, I decided to try another track.

"Listen, you remember free air."

"Sure. And I remember free toilets, too. But we don't have any public restrooms. That will probably be the next ordinance. We'll have to have free restrooms."

I decided to play my trump card and attack her conscience.

"Listen, what are you going to do if a kid pushes a bicycle up here with a flat tire and he doesn't have a quarter for the air hose?"

"Tell him to call his dad."

This time I really had her.

"But that's a pay phone over there. If the kid had a quarter for that. . . ."

"Oh, I'd let him use the phone back here . . . if he was a little gentleman about it and didn't start telling me that air should be free."

Just when I thought she was turning hostile, she smiled again.

"Kids will get by, mister. Believe me, they will."

"Even with pay toilets?"

"Did you ever climb over a partition?"

"Yes. I did, one time in a Greyhound bus station in Dallas."

"A kid will do that. And he'll do whatever. . . . Look out there, mister. See that kid with the bike?"

Sure enough, a boy with a bicycle was taking the last shot of air after a man had put air in an automobile tire. And then he rode happily away without paying anything.

Well, two can play that game.

I went outside, pulled my car over near the air vending machine and waited. Surely someone would come along pretty soon.

Changing Times
(gathered from a number of columns)

I'm not quite sure when technology became a scary subject with me, but it overtook me, passed me, embarrassed me. And I'll tell you about all of the times it happened.

Back in the early 1980s, someone invented a thing called a "touch lamp," and everybody had to have one. Remember? I'm not sure I was ready for such a lamp, but Marvalene bought one and took it home. Joe, then about ten, touched it until some thingamajig inside stopped working. I think that "touchless" lamp is still sitting in a dark closet somewhere in our house.

I'm not sure how that off-on switch worked, but folks told me that lightning would flip the switch. A lamp suddenly flashing on in the middle of the night is not my idea of a great invention, so I was thankful for Joe's help in this matter.

In 1986, attorney Frank Horne, a golfing companion, picked me up in one of those newfangled sports cars called a 300ZX. We were riding toward the golf course when a sultry female voice suddenly said, "You are low on fuel." I looked in the back seat to see who was there. "Who said that?" I asked.

"Technology at work," Frank said. And he explained his new car's features. "Well, let me out of this thing. I don't want to ride in a car that talks."

In 1989, Ma Bell introduced me to the computerized voice. I didn't know it at the time. I just punched in my credit card number to make a long-distance call, and a friendly voice said, "Thank you." I said, "You're welcome." Strangely, I didn't notice that it was the same voice, call after call, that said, "Thank you."

Finally, one day, Danny Gilleland, the *Telegraph*'s chief photographer was with me when I made a call and said, "You're welcome." He already knew about the newest technology. "You don't say 'Thank you' to that voice, you nut, that's a *computerized* voice."

Red-faced, I said, "Aw, I knew that. I was just seeing if you knew."

Danny teased me about it for months, and I think he told everyone in the newsroom about it.

Soon after that little innovation came something called "digital routing." You know what I'm talking about. You make a call and then get a voice that starts reeling off a directory like "Press 1 for the front desk, 2 for personnel, 3 for. . . ." It got so bad that, when I hear a real human voice these days, I feel like doing cartwheels . . . if I could indeed do cartwheels at my age.

We also suffered through another invention—soft drink machines that would talk to us. Joe actually looked for machines that would talk to him. Then a teenager, he mumbled something about being the first meaningful conversation he'd had all day. Of course, he wasn't talking about me.

In 1992, Mama got an answering machine, and I spent an hour on the phone trying to convince her that she should smash that thing to smithereens. "I hate answering machines, Mama. Am I supposed to call from Georgia to Arkansas to talk to a *machine?*"

"Well, you need to keep up with the times," she said, stopping short of calling me an old fuddy-duddy.

"Look, Mama, if you call me and I don't answer, it means *I ain't at home,* and you can call back later. That way, it doesn't cost you anything. Now, isn't that the best way?" "Well, I'm keeping my answering machine," said my eighty-one-year-old Mama. And she did.

Danny Gilleland was one of the first at the *Telegraph* to get a cellular phone. We were riding to Milledgeville one day when that thing went off and Ol' Boyd nearly jumped out of his skin. We had a round about cell phones, and I told him that I wasn't riding with anyone who had one of those things going off all the time. He said, "Well, it's been fun, Ol' Boyd."

Of course, I went with him again. We were a great team, and I wasn't going to let a little old telephone break up a productive partnership. Eventually, I got my own cell phone. It was the quick and easy way, especially after AT&T busted up and those Mickey Mouse companies started denying my calling card number. And right now, I wonder how I ever got along without a cell phone. (Never thought I'd say that, but it's true. Just don't tell Danny.)

Don't think that I'm down on technology. Shoot, I've got hearing aids in both ears—stereo, you know—and they are little bitty things that contain some of the best technology in the world. These fit way down in the ear, and that is especially nice. You may remember I warned people who wear hearing aids to watch out for lovers who like to lick your ear. They'll short out your circuits and light you up like a pinball machine.

Well, dear friends, there's one invention to which I have *not* surrendered—the ATM. I know you're not going to believe this, but if I can hold out for a few more months, I will enter a new millennium without *ever* having drawn money out of an automatic teller machine.

Old-fashioned, is that what you're thinking? It's all right. Some of us change very slowly.

O Say, Can You Sing?
(from a column published on January 27, 1997)

While waiting to make a speech recently, I listened as the man at the microphone said we were going to sing "The Star-Spangled Banner." Since that is the No. 1 song for all red-white-and-blue Americans, I was happy to join in. I forgot momentarily that it is a very difficult song to sing.

I'd like to be able to sing "The Star-Spangled Banner" more than any other song in the world, but I just can't hack it. On that day, however, I tried. And the lady next to me jumped like she'd just heard a wolf howl in her ear. Her face scrooched up and her head wagged in disapproval.

Was I off key? Of course, I was. It's the only key I know. So I gave her a break. I sang the rest of it under my breath.

Now I don't know who is responsible for mailing me a yellowed clipping about how people can't sing our National Anthem, but I suspect it was the lady standing next to me the other day. The clipping, taken from the *Los Angeles Times*, told how singers and musical groups are chosen to sing or play "The Star-Spangled Banner" at Anaheim Stadium, home of the California Angels baseball team.

Hundreds of people and groups audition for the chance. Hundreds! Of course, some don't have to audition. I'll bet Johnny Mathis didn't. Or Glen Campbell. Or the Lettermen. But Dr. Mark Miller is a singer who did it the hard way. Funny thing, Mark Miller once auditioned for the "Ed Sullivan Show." After listening, Sullivan's booking agent reportedly said, "You know, you're a nice Jewish kid. Why don't you go to medical school and become a doctor?" He did just that. He became a cardiologist. But he never lost his ambition to sing, so he auditioned for the honor of singing "The Star-Spangled Banner" in Anaheim Stadium. On that occasion, he wasn't told to become a doctor.

In fact, he sang it in front of 65,000 fans. Ironically, it was "Bat Day" at the stadium, and Dr. Miller, who still wasn't 100 percent sure of his ability, said, "Can you imagine singing a song as difficult as 'The Star-Spangled Banner' to 65,000 people with bats in their hands?"

One thing that Dr. Miller, Glen Campbell and the others have in common is that they have to perform free at the Angels' game. But enough about where it's sung. I want to talk about how it's sung.

Professional singer Helen Hudson, who divides her time between Los Angeles and New York, has sung the national anthem before games for the Angels, the New York Mets, the New York Knicks, and the Los Angeles Dodgers. "If you can sing the national anthem," she said, "it shows your whole range. It separates the men from the boys." Seems like an odd quote for a lady to make, but okay, I think it explains my problem. My voice just never grew up.

And, of course, no other song evokes the jitters in a singer like our national anthem. Johnny Mathis, holder of sixty gold records, once said, "Singing it is like a centipede trying to decide which leg to move next. You're not quite sure you know the words. It's a very strange feeling." That's another problem I have with the song. Goose bumps always stand up on me and I get the jitters when I (try to) sing it. Centipedes give me a fit, too.

The late Nat King Cole, one of my all-time favorites, once admitted he forgot the words in front of a World Series crowd packed into old Dodger Stadium. He never did say whether he just let the music play or if he hummed along.

Say, maybe that's the answer. All of us non-singers should just hum along. Let's try it. Hmm-hmm-hm-hm-hm-hmmm. I think we're going to have a problem with "the rocket's red glare" and "the bombs bursting in air." But if it can shake up Johnny Mathis and Nat King Cole, what are off-key singers like you and me supposed to do?

Ferry Good Memories
(from a column published on June 28, 1995)

MARSHALLVILLE—The man stood at the edge of the river and looked around. Paradise was surely lost, he thought. How long had it been since he first came to this peaceful spot once known as the Flint River Ferry? Twenty years? Longer? His son had been very young in those days. He'd held the tot's hand so he would not wander too close to the swift-flowing water.

"Want to cross?" the father asked.

"On that boat?" the boy said.

"On the boat."

"Yes!"

"Then let's honk the horn."

Together, they pushed the button that would bring the operator out of the gray house on the cliff and down the steps to the roadway. The operator of the Flint River Ferry was a friendly man who shook hands with the boy and asked if he was ready to cross. The boy uttered another excited "Yes!" and they were on the way. And it was a ride to remember. Maybe not as exciting as the boy's first Little League home run, but close.

Once on the other side, the man drove the car off the ferry and turned it around. The ferry operator waited. He'd done this countless times. People brought their children here to experience a real river ferry crossing. It was the last one in Georgia at the time. The operator understood. The man's mind wandered back to another time, when it was cheaper to operate a ferry than it was to build a sturdy bridge. Some folks complained about ferries. They were useless when the river was at flood stage, critics said, and much slower than crossing a bridge. The world was in a hurry, it seemed.

The man and his son returned a number of times after that first visit and on one occasion, the operator even let the boy push the handle that engaged the engine and moved the ferry along a cable to the other side. The man loved the ferry so much that he bought an artist's rendering of the scene and hung it in his home so he could stand on that river bank any time he wanted.

The boy grew up. By the time the state revealed plans to bypass the ferry with a bridge that would cost almost $4 million, the boy was hitting home runs in high school. Father and son never came back to the ferry together.

Seven years ago, a gray ribbon of asphalt and a concrete bridge put the ferry out of business. The state transportation department didn't need it any more. Not only were there no funds to keep it operational for tourists, the man knew very well that the ferry would never make it as a tourist attraction. It was too remote, too far from the superhighways. How can you convince someone whizzing along an interstate highway to detour twenty miles just to ride on something that looks like it belonged in the 1800s?

The ferry made its last crossing in 1988. Then it was disassembled and taken to a museum. The ramp where cars once loaded on the ferry is now just a boat ramp. The gray house where ferry operators once lived is now a private home. Vines clutter the steps leading up the cliff.

Standing by the river on a hot summer day, the man had an urge. He walked to his car and honked the horn. Of course, nobody came. But it felt good to make the sound that once brought Homer Cromer or Lester Cromer or Wiley Jones down to the ferry. The man could almost see and hear the ghosts:

- The many picnickers with laughing, playful children

- A senior couple that once was shocked by skinny-dippers a couple of hundred yards downstream from the ferry
- A bride and groom and minister floating on the ferry as the couple were married
- The scattering of the ashes of an old man who'd desired such a resting place, . . . and the murmur of a mourner on the ferry who said, "He'll be in Albany by Thursday."

The man listened for a moment, took one last look around before he got in his car and drove away. Yes, the ferry was gone. His son was all grown up. And paradise was surely lost.

Blacksmithing...
Still an Honorable Profession
(from a column published on January 24, 1993)

HAWKINSVILLE—Standing in the midst of many years of left-over parts and scrap iron in the old blacksmith shop, I asked a question: "How long have you been here?" Russell Harris cocked an eye toward the blackened ceiling and said, "Oh, a little more than two hundred years."

Of course, Russell isn't two hundred years old. It's just that when you discuss the blacksmith shop with him, he feels obliged to talk for the other Harrises who practiced the blacksmith trade there: his father, his grandfather, his great-grandfather and his great-great grandfather.

That's right, Russell is the fifth generation to work in that shop. His son, Terry, is the sixth, and Russell wouldn't be surprised if one of his grandsons takes up the trade, too. The way he figures it, there's no better way for a person to make a living than working for himself, doing what makes him happy, and being around people he likes.

About fifteen years ago Russell Harris used an old forge behind the shop to do much of his work. I asked about it this time, and he showed it to me. Obviously, it had been idle for a long time. "It'll still work," he reassured me. "All I'd have to do is fire it up. The bellows are right there inside the shop."

Of course, I knew he wasn't going to fire it up. Modern tools like arc welders and cutting torches make jobs easier and quicker these days. Besides that, Russell will turn seventy-nine on March 20, and even though he doesn't like to talk about the years slipping away, he isn't as agile or quick as he used to be.

There are some other things, besides fixing a plow blade or mending an axle, that seem important to him these days. For instance, he likes his fire on a cold and rainy day. He builds it in a two-foot-high piece of steel about as big around as an oil drum. His fuel is scrap lumber.

He likes his friends. Vernon Collier was there. So was Lucious Bray. Even the mailman, James Laidlar, paused to visit a few minutes as he delivered the day's mail.

And Russell likes the conversation. For instance, there was an exchange about who'd known him the longest.

"I've been coming here for forty-five years," said Lucious Bray.

Dumb me, I asked, "And how old are you?"

"Forty-five," he said.

Russell gestured to the mailman and said, "I used to work on his granddaddy's mules, didn't I?"

"Yep," said James Laidlar, "and Grandpa's been dead since 1941. Now that was a while ago."

But the younger men had a losing cause when it came to longevity. Russell nodded toward Vernon Collier. "Now, that fellow and I go *way* back. I remember when he worked for me for fifty cents a day."

Vernon nodded, "Yes, sir, I did that, but it was back when fifty cents would buy a lot of bread and milk."

Russell rocked forward on his tractor-seat-made-into-a-chair and looked out at the splattering raindrops. "Ain't gonna be nothing moving today," he said. "When the farmers can't work, we can't work." No one complained. "You know," Russell said, "this place is getting to be just like an old folks home."

What about Terry, the sixth generation blacksmith, I asked.

"Oh, he's got a regular job at the (cotton) mill down yonder," he said. "He works here when there's nothing going on down there."

Conversation ranged from drugs (despised in that shop) to prayer in school (they favor it) to wearing blue jeans to church (they like that idea, too) to the economy ("it's an awful mess").

Someone jogged Russell's memory about how he used to leave Hawkinsville to find more work, and Russell told us how he followed the cotton harvesting season from Whatley, Georgia, to Big Spring, Texas, to work on gins. "I did some traveling, but I always came back here," he said of the old shop. "If I had to stay away from here more than six or eight months at one time, I might as well be dead." The others nodded, knowing their friend had spoken the gospel truth.

I noticed a huge anvil sitting off to one side and I asked about it. "Now, there's a story behind that anvil," Russell said. I was betting on it. "When I went to get that anvil . . . well, I didn't have a truck back then, so I cut the back end off an old car and built me a platform. Then I drove all the way to Dania, Florida to get it. I paid forty-five dollars for it but that was a long time ago. An anvil like that will sell for seven dollars a pound these days." And how much does it weigh? "Better than 150 pounds." I whistled. That was a lot of dough—or steel.

Russell gestured to tools hanging on the walls. "I've got the things to work on wagon wheels and buggy wheels," he said. "But ain't none of it for sale. I don't know what the kids will do with it when I'm gone, but none of it's for sale right now."

Finally, he sat back down on the old tractor seat and warmed his hands by the fire. "Sure is a messy day. Just ain't much good for anything except maybe hanging around this old folks home." The others nodded agreement. And they watched the rain fall.

5

CHARACTERS I HAVE KNOWN

W hen I try to call the roll
of characters I have known, I find that most of them have
gone on to that special place where storytellers and good
listeners gather in the hereafter. And I get a little sad. On the
other hand, if it hadn't been for the characters I've known,
life would have been pretty dull. In fact, I wonder what the
next generation is going to do for characters. Who is going to
entertain and enlighten the younger folks? Television? The
Internet? Well, you can scan the dial and surf the Internet,
but until you've heard a country boy like Muley talk about
hunting dogs or shooting marbles or hear a lady like Miss
Myrt, proprietress of a used book store, ask the tough questions in life . . . well, as Miss Myrt would say, "Honey, you
ain't living it up!" I invite you to live it up with some characters I have known.

Muley
The Country Boy

Muley was truly a best friend. He came into my life one morning in the snack bar at the *Macon Telegraph* building. Someone already had pointed him out to me as the man who signed our paychecks. An old Marine habit made me want to get acquainted with him (Marines who had friends in the disbursing office seldom had pay problems).

It didn't take long for me to discover that I'd stumbled onto one of the most interesting characters I'd ever know. His real name was Howard Durwood Rainey. Most people called him Durwood. I did, too, at first. By the time my first column went to press in 1977, Durwood and I were fast friends. Both of us were morning people. I once asked Muley about the peak of his day. (I thought he might say coffee time with me.) He said, "Well, I'm gettin' older, so I guess it comes pretty early. Like when my feet hit the floor in the morning. From there, it's all downhill." As I got older, I discovered he'd spoken a lot of truth.

Muley also had a different take on issues. For instance, when Atlanta Braves star pitcher Pascual Perez was locked up in the Dominican Republic for possessing cocaine, we were sitting around the Liar's Table that morning talking bad about Perez. Muley listened as he got a cup of coffee and sat down, and then he said. "You guys are wrong. I *like* Perez."

Of course, we got on his case. How could he possibly like someone who was such a poor role model for our young? "Well," Muley drawled, "he's the only person I know who's carrying that junk *out* of this country. Load him up and let him fly!"

As the conversation turned to cathead biscuits, whittling, and earrings for men, Muley always took a stand and no one could jar him away from it. Problem is, he always seemed to be right. But his stubbornness was the thing that caused me to start calling him Muley—for being so mule-headed, of course.

He became my sounding board as well as a source of columns and wisdom and humor. Even a short conversation with him could turn into a column—from shooting marbles and farming hogs to bypass surgery and love for a grandson. Muley became my best friend in another way. I could discuss *anything* with him and feel at ease. He never came close to betraying a confidence. I know that for sure. As much as I confided in him, if he'd slipped up, I surely would have known.

Well, he did tell on me one time. He pointed to my shoes and said, "Ol' Boyd is so good at flea marketing that he bought one of those shoes in South Carolina and then went to Alabama and found an exact match." But I quickly forgave him. You see, I got a column out of it.

After he retired, Muley traveled a lot of miles with me. Every sight, every sound, every human being reminded him of something worth talking about. As we talked, more columns came together. Muley contributed to so many columns that I once told him I might just start running a mug shot of a mule at the top of the column and call it "Muley's Mutterings." Hearing that idea, he grinned like a mule munching briars.

But sometimes, he'd turn down a chance to ride the backroads. "My grandboy is over here, and we've got some plans for the day," he'd say. I understand his dedication to his grandsons a lot more now that I have one of my own.

Muley made friends wherever he went. He'd sometimes accompany me to speeches, but he'd never make a speech himself. If asked, he'd gesture toward me and say, "He's the guy with all the fancy words."

And, as his name became a household word, he never tried to capitalize on it in any way. Except for the Over-75 Party each October, he shied away from public appearances. Even so, he could work a crowd better than any politician.

Muley died in the fall of 1998, and he drew his last breath among friends. He was sitting in his favorite restaurant, laughing at Cowboy Tatum's admission that he'd paid $1,000 for a hunting dog to track a legendary wild boar in South Georgia, when he collapsed and died. I'm glad he lived past my own retirement. I never could have written four columns a week without him.

There's an emptiness in me now that is hard to describe. I found out about that a few days after his death. Missiles were raining down on terrorist bases half a world away, and I knew he would have an observation or two. His perspective would make a lot more sense than anything those slicked-up talking heads on TV had to say. I actually reached for the phone before it hit me: Muley ain't here anymore. His absence makes me appreciate—more than ever—the best friends I still have.

Miss Myrt
Asks the Tough Questions
(from a column published on October 2, 1987)

I stopped by to see Miss Myrt the other day, never dreaming I might be in trouble with one of my favorite people. Early in autumn, the front door of her book store stood open, beckoning like an old friend. How many times have I gone there? A hundred. Maybe more. But every visit is like a tonic, a break from worry and work.

Myrt Collier was sitting in her easy chair under the breeze of a fan. Garfield, the calico cat that took up residence at the book store nearly a year ago, was snoozing under a table. "Well, well, well," she said, "look who's here." Obediently, Garfield raised his head, looked at me almost disdainfully and then went back to sleep. "So you finally remembered your way home, did you?" Miss Myrt asked.

Somehow, her greeting reminded me of my Mama's tone when her son was a little late getting home from playing at the school playground. "I've been real busy, Miss Myrt," I said in the same apologetic tone I once used toward my irate Mama.

"Well, sit down," she said, "and tell me what you found out."

"Found out? About what?"

"You know."

I searched my mind. Was I supposed to find out something?

"You drew a blank," she said.

I nodded.

"You were supposed to find out why we Americans think the Easter bunny can lay eggs." Oh, yes. The Easter bunny. Gee, it *had* been a long time since I'd visited with Miss Myrt.

"I didn't find out," I confessed. She fixed me with a steady gaze. "Did you know you've driven me to drink?"

That shocked me. Miss Myrt wouldn't drink enough to keep a titmouse tanked. "Naw," I said in disbelief.

"Sure you did," she said. "Just the other day, me and some friends got together and I asked them about the Easter bunny. I said that you were supposed to find out but I hadn't heard from you in ages."

"Gee, I'm sorry. But how did this drive you to drink?"

"Well, all of us got to talking and trying to figure it out. We couldn't but since it was a hot day, we started eating snow cones. And then someone said that maybe a little rum in the snow cones would make our minds work better. So we ate rum snow cones."

"Did that help?"

"We never did figure out why the Easter bunny lays eggs, but after about four snow cones, it didn't seem to matter anymore."

I sighed with relief.

"But it matters now. I still want to know."

"Miss Myrt, you ask some pretty tough questions."

"I'm ready and willing to answer *your* tough questions."

"Like what?"

"Just ask me one, and I'll show you."

"Well, uh. . ."

"Go ahead."

"Well, OK. Why doesn't someone make a deodorant that smells like money?"

"They're trying to protect people like you."

"Huh?"

"It's as plain as the nose on your face. If you went around smelling like money, someone would knock you over the head and steal everything you've got. Folks who make deodorant are just trying to protect people like you."

"Oh."

"Do you have another question?"

"Hmmm . . . Okay, I've got one. You know how people go for exotic coffee. There are all kinds of flavors—cinnamon, Irish creme, hazelnut. How come someone doesn't come up with a coffee that tastes like grits?"

Miss Myrt clucked her tongue at me and shook her head. "Don't you know that grits are tasteless? The only thing you taste in grits is butter. Leave the butter out and there's no taste. So why make a coffee that doesn't taste like anything at all?"

Garfield raised his head and looked sadly at me.

"Now," said Miss Myrt, "it's your turn. When do I find out about the Easter bunny?"

I left her place feeling pretty dumb. I still don't know why we keep brainwashing our children that the Easter bunny laid the eggs that we hide in the yard each spring.

Willie Bob Martin
My Attitude Adjuster
(gathered from a dozen columns)

I met him, oh, must have been a dozen years ago, maybe more. He shined my shoes and added a genuine smile for a buck and a half. Is that a deal or what? I kept going back to Genone's Barber shop to see Willie Bob Martin because I needed to talk to him.

He was my "attitude adjuster." A conversation with Willie Bob would let me know that my town had something more than crime and drugs and self-serving politicians. This man was an island of kindness in a town that could always use another dab. Willie Bob could tell a story in the time that it takes to shine two shoes, and he would take me back to a time when. . . .

Almost seventy years ago, Willie Bob went to work in Warfield Stables in Macon. He was as good at handling mules and breaking horses as anyone who ever worked there, some of the oldtimers told me. A compassionate soul, Willie Bob earned the nickname of "Long Boy" because he led a sick horse nine miles from the other side of Dry Branch to downtown Macon. He had switched horses with a farmer, and other handlers might have chosen to ride the sick horse back to town. But not Willie Bob.

When the tide of tractors closed the stables, Willie Bob went to work as a meatcutter at T&T Packing. Although he could neither read nor write, he persevered by memorizing the labels. According to those who knew him back then, he never used the wrong label. He worked in each of those places for twenty-some years. By the time fire destroyed T&T twenty-three years ago,

Willie Bob was old enough to retire. But he wasn't ready to just quit, so he started shining shoes at Genone's.

The barber shop was the perfect place for his stories, and he kept us laughing with tales about breaking more than 300 horses in his younger days. He always recalled those days with unabashed delight.

One time, he showed me a picture of himself holding the reins on a Shetland pony with a young girl in the saddle. He wondered what had ever happened to the girl. I figured our readers would know, so we published the picture and we located her in Atlanta. They had a happy reunion in 1994.

Some folks said that I made a lot of friends for Willie Bob by writing about him. But it was really the other way around. He made a lot of friends for me.

How many friends did Willie Bob have? Zillions. Several years ago, I mentioned that his birthday was coming up, and friends brought him four birthday cakes. He had all of those friends because he knew how to get along with others. And he got along because he seldom took sides in everyday disputes.

My friend wasn't easily led. When two men in the barber shop tried to draw him into a political debate, Willie Bob wouldn't have any of it.

"I handle that just like I used to handle horses," he said. "I'd get those reins in my hands, and I'd hold him in the middle of the road. I do that with them (the men in the shop). I stay right in the middle of the road . . . unless there's a good reason to take sides, of course."

A couple of years ago, his wife and only child died within a few days of each other, and we all grieved with him. Later, Willie Bob began losing weight. When I asked about it, he told me that he had prostate cancer. Still, he came to the shop every day, shined shoes and swapped stories. I kept thinking, "This man will outlive us all."

In mid-December, I stopped at Genone's, only to learn that Willie Bob was out sick. "It's bad," said barber Grover Spillers. "I don't think he will ever come back to work."

The Boyds went to visit, and Wonderful Wanda, the college student who'd never hung around the barber shop, soon became Willie Bob's special buddy. She took him meals and ran errands until his granddaughter, Angela Rawls, could move in and look after him. After one visit, Wanda, with tears in her eyes, said to me, "I love that old man."

"We all do," I said.

Willie Bob made one last comeback. He drove himself to the barber shop and shined a few pairs of shoes. But then his strength began to ebb, and Willie Bob Martin, a true gentleman in every respect, and the smartest man I ever knew who could neither read nor write, died peacefully in his bed on March 5, 1995.

I lost a great friend.

Chess McCartney
The Legendary Goat Man
(from columns that appeared in 1979, 1985 and 1997)

I don't remember any of my elderly friends laying black skid marks with the wheels on their walkers, but that was the reaction of the Goat Man (in 1997) when I asked if he wanted to visit his homeplace near Jeffersonville. Funny thing, he came into an interview room at Eastview Nursing Center looking like a tired old legend who was simply consenting to one more string of questions. His gait was slow and his interest was focused only on a recent book about his unusual life.

Then I said something about home and the old guy's eyes sparkled like a kid's on Christmas morn. He left that room like it was on fire. I wouldn't say there was a spring in his step, but there certainly was a purpose to his shuffle.

Riding out the highway toward Jeffersonville, he looked at the scene and said, "Sure is a pretty day." The Goat Man, alias Chess McCartney, can appreciate those sunny, blue-sky days more than you and I because he has seen more of them and probably has considerably fewer left. How many blue skies has the Goat Man gazed upon? Well, his birthday is coming up on July 6, and how many birthdays he's seen depends on who's talking.

The Goat Man says it's 107. His only child, Albert Gene McCartney, age sixty-one, says it's 105. I have a pamphlet he wrote during the Eisenhower administration that implies that he's ninety-six. But, given his longevity, let's allow him to be any age he wants, okay?

Charles "Chess" McCartney was born on July 6, 1901, according to a book he once peddled to tourists for fifty cents a copy. A twin brother died at birth. His early years were spent in Van Buren County, Iowa, but in 1915, at the age of fourteen, he hit the road. And he didn't truly give up life on the road until he went into a nursing home in 1987.

When I came to this area, the Goat Man was already a legend. He was living along U.S. 80 a few miles west of Jeffersonville. There was no problem finding him. Folks in Jeffersonville gave specific directions: Go out the main highway a good piece (in rural Georgia, that's about five miles), keep looking left until you see a couple of school bus bodies down in a hollow (in Georgia, that's "holler").

There was no problem interviewing him, either. He had hosted scores of media folks over the years. Even though none of them ever asked to stay overnight, the Goat Man always asked them to "stick around," even when daylight was fading fast. Of course, I had seen postcards of him with a ramshackle wagon and a team of a dozen goats or more. But when I met him, he had just two friends with hooves—a goat named Barbara and a pony named Ladybird. He patiently answered all my questions about his settling here in the 1940s, about his subsequent wandering, about being a minister and building a small chapel that had burned down.

Stories about him filled a file in the newsroom library. One of them says he traveled more than 100,000 miles by goat train, from Florida and Maine to Washington and California. He went thirty-six years at one time without ever sleeping in a house or in a bed. He once announced that he was running for president, but he stepped aside in favor of a young man named John F. Kennedy.

His life story had been told and retold in dozens of cities. People sometimes gathered almost like it was a holiday parade to watch the Goat Man pass through. He braved even the worst of weather conditions, and he described for me how many goats it took to keep him warm. "On a one-goat night, it's just about freezing," he said. "On a five-goat night, it's below zero." When anyone criticized the goat-like odor that followed him everywhere, the Goat Man had a ready reply: "I ain't got no banker's job."

In spite of that, the Goat Man found compassionate people wherever he went. One Christmas near Ringgold, Georgia, about twenty good-hearted people showed up bearing plates piled high with food. Even the goats ate well on that night, he told me.

In 1969, the Goat Man told reporters that he was quitting the road. His home was a few acres of land in Twiggs County where the McCartneys first settled in the 1940s. His mother and stepfather are buried there. It would always be his home, he said.

He shared a little shack there with his only son, Albert Gene, until it burned in the early 1970s. Then he brought in the bodies of two school buses. Even though there was no running water, he made do. When a woman asked how long it had been since he'd had a bath, he huffed and said, "Probably when my parents gave me one." Through the 1970s, the Goat Man and Albert Gene, sometimes called "Goat Boy," could be seen walking the highways, picking up aluminum cans.

Then bad things began happening to the Goat Man. He became entangled in a rope tied to Ladybird, and, when the pony bolted, his arm was injured seriously enough that he had to make one of his rare visits to a doctor.

When his shack burned, he barely escaped. First- and second-degree burns put him in a "rest home" for a while. But he promised to "bust out of this joint" if they didn't voluntarily release him. Somehow, they kept him until his injuries were pretty much healed and then he went home and bought the school bus bodies to replace the shack.

And he hit the road again. In late 1985, he simply disappeared. Even Albert Gene said he didn't have a clue about where his father had gone. A huge search was launched before he finally turned up in Los Angeles. He said he'd gone there to see Morgan Fairchild. He said she wanted to marry him, but the actress never confirmed any romantic ties. In 1987, his physical condition deteriorated. He suffered from dehydration, and two toes were amputated when gangrene caused by frostbite set in. The folks at Eastview got him just in time.

Ten years have passed, and the considerable strength the Goat Man had when I first met him has slipped away. His steps are merely a shuffle of what they used to be, and he's nearly deaf. But he heard me when I said something about going home. So we went. With assistance, he made his way down a roadside embankment, along a narrow pathway through underbrush and into the clearing around the two school bus bodies that were once his home.

Albert Gene was there, kicking the ever-present aluminum cans out of the way so his father could get a closer look at the place. Then I asked the Goat Man if he remembered the place. He shook his head. "No, I don't," he said.

"But you know that fellow, don't you?" I asked.

At first, he didn't answer. At age ninety-six and after ten years in a nursing home, maybe a person can forget what home once looked like. But forget his own son? Finally, he looked at the Goat Boy and said, "Albert Gene, your whiskers are getting gray!"

On the trip back to town, the Goat Man didn't say much. He didn't even bother to say that it was a nice day. But maybe he was just remembering, and maybe he didn't want to share his thoughts. After all, not too many people ever understood the man or the way he lived. Isn't it a little late now?

(Footnote: The Goat Man died in 1997. His son, Albert Gene, was murdered a few months later.)

Bert and Ott
Twin Sisters Forever
(from a column published on October 13, 1995)

MONTROSE—Everybody is on an individuality kick these days. Tell someone he or she looks like someone else, and that person will immediately get a new hair style or a face lift. Have you noticed that even twins seldom look alike these days? Or want to? Don't expect twin sisters Bert Payne or Ott Cannon to act like that, however. They still look very much alike and they always dress alike—right down to identical necklaces and earrings—when they go out. More than that, each is still the other's best friend. All this after ninety-two years. Yes, I said ninety-two years.

This pair has been a delight for the Over-75 Party ever since that first party was held in 1983. I thought about the twins the other day, and it dawned on me that even though I've known them for a dozen years and have mentioned them in this column a dozen times or more, I'd never really heard their story. So I found them and I listened to their story about a lasting, loving, good-times sort of sisterhood.

They were born Elberta and Elliot Cook, the second and third children of Joel and Dollie Cook. Their names were soon shortened to Bert and Ott, and they still answer to those nicknames. Their parents farmed about 1,300 acres and also operated several businesses, including a store, a sawmill and a cotton gin. Given women's roles at the time, it stands to reason that the girls didn't really *have* to work in the fields. But they did. "They'd much rather have been in the fields with their daddy than washing dishes," says Mae Merritt, one of Bert's three children. "They weren't the kind to stay inside."

And they were always very close. If you found one, you would usually find the other. It was that way the day they saw their first automobile.

Dr. James B. Duggan, the man who delivered the twins, drove the first car through Cooktown, a small community about six miles east of Allentown. The girls heard about that newfangled contraption, but they couldn't get a glimpse of it. So they devised a scheme. They worked together to make a huge pile of sand in the road near their house, and sure enough, the old country doctor soon came chugging down the road in his new car. Of course, he had to stop and shovel that pile of sand down far enough that he could drive over it. While he shoveled sand, the girls gawked at the car.

If someone suggests that perhaps the twins didn't do the *hard* work, like picking cotton, Bert quickly puts that notion to rest. "I'll bet I did pick cotton!" she said emphatically. "I picked 150 pounds in a day one time."

Each of them married, Bert when she was seventeen and Ott when she was twenty-three. Bert bore three daughters in her marriage to Floral Payne, and Ott gave birth to one girl and three boys in her marriage to Hardy B. Cannon.

Neither of the sisters ever lived more than a couple of miles from the homeplace except one time. Bert worked at Robins Air Force Base during the war and lived in Warner Robins for slightly less than one year.

Did their togetherness foster any disagreements? "We've never been mad at each other," Ott said. "We love each other too much to get mad."

Did they always dress alike? "Always," they said in unison. Even after they were grown, they never grew tired of it. In fact, when one of the twins sees a dress that she likes, she simply buys two.

Does one ever buy something the other doesn't like? "No," they said, again almost simultaneously. Any time they are going out together, one of them will call the other and they will discuss what to wear, right down to the trimmings.

Does the identity of these twins sometimes confuse others like younger identical twins do? Of course. When both were hospitalized several years ago, they sent a young physical therapist's head into a spin. The therapist saw Bert on one floor and then went directly to a room on the next floor and found Ott in another room. Naturally, he wondered how someone three times his age and who needed physical therapy could move up to the next floor faster than the elevator he'd ridden.

Who is the leader of the two? Bert gestured to Ott and said, "I listen to her. She was born first (by about five minutes)."

After their parents died, the twins continued to run the farm, Mae Merritt said. "Mama always preferred a pickup," she said. "She would haul hogs to market and do all sorts of chores." And any time a conversation like that comes up, someone is sure to tell a story or two about the early days. Like the time Bert was driving a horse and wagon and failed to negotiate a turn. Family members explode in laughter as Ott's son, Joe Cannon, tells about how she hung up the wagon on a stump. Tales like that one are told and re-told and become part of a family lore for future generations.

Both of the twins are widows now, and they know that time is taking its toll on them, too. Maybe that's why the twins are closer than ever. At a recent gathering of twins, Bert tried to explain their closeness by saying she hoped that, since they were born together and spent so many years together, it would be fitting if they would pass on at the same time.

What Bert didn't know was that the television cameras were rolling and the big-city media thought that was a perfect example of the love of twin sisters. And they put it on the air. Bert listened as family members recounted that incident, and then she said it again: "You know that isn't going to happen. But it would be okay with me." Isn't that what you might expect her to say after ninety-two years?

Joe Pruett
The Two-Liner Man
(from a column published in 1987

Joe F. Pruett is one of the few admitted thieves I'll claim as a friend. But all of us need the bits of humor he steals and assembles in a loose-leaf notebook. Listen: *How many legs does a centipede have to lose to limp?* You'll notice this smile fits in just two lines in his slender little books. So do some 1,800 others he has collected. If Joe has to, he rewrites them to fit in a column thirty-nine picas wide—about sixty-five characters on a typewriter. Examples: *It costs more to amuse a kid than it did to educate his father. Any experience that doesn't kill you will make you stronger. If you don't mind that your kids don't mind, your kids won't mind.*

Young Joe Pruett grew up in Lee County near Albany. At age twelve, he became editor of the *Lee County Journal* (now the *Lee County Ledger*). That's no misprint. I said age twelve. In the sixty-seven years since then, there has hardly been a time when Joe was not meeting a deadline for some type of publication. Most of the time, he has had a hand in several. Now at age seventy-nine, he is busily engaged in publishing the *Golden Times*, the printed voice of the Macon chapter of the AARP, and the *Veep*, a Sunday School publication of Vineville Presbyterian Church. He also contributes columns to the *Lee County Ledger* and the *Exchangite*, the Georgia Exchange Club's statewide publication. "I can't remember when I wasn't getting out some kind of publication," he said.

Those early years in Leesburg set the pace for his life. By the time he graduated from high school, he already had four years of newspaper experience. He moved to Atlanta in 1923 to attend Georgia Tech, but dropped out in a matter of weeks and went to work for a candy company. For the next eight years, he didn't have a hand in publishing a newspaper or newsletter.

In 1931, he moved to Louisville, Kentucky, and began publishing *The Optimist* for International Harvester, a farm equipment manufacturer. As Joe remembers, "It was during the Depression, and everyone was down. I tried to lift them up a little."

In 1935 he moved to Macon. He still worked for International Harvester, but he says that was the year he last punched a time clock. He "retired" about ten years ago, but he's slowed down very little.

"I get up every morning looking for things to do," he says. One thing he does regularly is add to his collection of two-liners. Many were newspaper fillers at one time. But if Joe hears something he likes and it is a little too long, he'll find a way to shorten it so it fits in just two lines. He readily gives credit where credit is due. "Stolen from others by Joe F. Pruett" is his hallmark. That credit line appears on his four twelve-page pamphlets titled *A Lot Can Be Said in Just Two Lines*. Each of the booklets contains about 200 of his sayings.

His booklets have found their way into thousands of hands because he sends them instead of Christmas or get-well cards. I'm sure they've brought a smile where a smile was needed most. In fact, I found one that must have been written especially for Joe Pruett:

Smiles never go up in price or down in value.
So go ahead. Smile.

Emory Wilcox
A melon and a blessing
(from a column published in 1994)

FITZGERALD—It's been a long time since I bought a cantaloupe that was "a blessing." Maybe I've never made such a buy . . . until the other day. Emory Wilcox said it would be a blessing if I bought one because the money he makes at the fruit stand in front of his house helps him to keep on spreading God's word. When I heard that, I bought two. That's when he threw in an extra one as "a blessing." Three 'lopes for two bucks and a blessing, too? It was my day, folks.

Yes, sir, it'll always be a blessing that I met this eighty-two-year-old preacher. Besides being a pretty good produce salesman, Brother Wilcox can spread God's word without offending. It takes a special person to do that, don't you think?

You've met hard-line (and hard-headed) Christians who say you get to Heaven their way or no way. And you've met people who just talk about religion and wouldn't know the Second Coming if it happened in their living room.

Brother Wilcox and I fit in somewhere between those two groups. And we agree on something else. Deeds are more important than spoken words. Brother Wilcox lives his religion day by day and preaches almost constantly. Let me tell you about him.

Emory Wilcox was born in 1912, "just about seven miles back out there in the woods," he said, waving a hand eastward. His memories of life on a farm wouldn't impress today's young folk. "I had one pair of shoes," he said, "and I felt lucky to have that. I plowed in them and then cleaned 'em good on Saturday night so I could wear 'em to church. I had one pair of good pants and I washed them out on Saturday, too." That's the way he came up—poor but proud.

He left the farm and he left Georgia in 1931. He was just nineteen when he made his way to Miami and became a house painter. He says he became a very good one. "I didn't use cheap material and I didn't do cheap work," he said. "After a while, people would call me and tell me to paint their house, and they didn't ask how much I was going to charge."

In 1934, he came back home long enough to marry Ara Jay of Fitzgerald and move her to Miami, too.

Brother Wilcox says he was past his thirtieth birthday when he felt the call to preach. Since then, he has never let it rest. In all, he has pastored just five churches, and right now, he leads the flock at The Church of the Kingdom of God.

About twelve years ago, he returned to his hometown and bought a house at the corner of Main and Ohoopee streets, a few blocks north of Fitzgerald's business district. Brother Wilcox has "done a little peddling ever since I came back (to Fitzgerald)," and then, a couple of years ago, he put up a few tables under a huge shade tree in his front yard and started selling fresh fruit and vegetables. But I think he spreads God's word faster than he sells produce.

He looked at me as I picked out my cantaloupes and said, "Joy, joy, joy. I can see it in your face, brother, and that's good. Joy drives the Devil away. He can't stand joy." Should I have told Brother Wilcox that it was *he* who put that happy smile on my face? No, he would have said any joy I felt surely came from above. So I didn't bother.

With two cantaloupes in the back seat and him going after the "blessing" cantaloupe, I looked him over. His red suspenders made him look younger, not older, than his eighty-two years, and his shoes were stuff of which novelists write. The toes were knocked out to a comfortable degree, and his feet looked like they could actually breathe on that hot summer day.

As he put the third 'lope in the back seat, he said, "That's your blessing. . . . Where'd you say you were from? Macon? Well, I'll reach you again, brother. Not by telephone, but by the spirit."

We were talking about family and he was telling me about his only child, Virginia, who lives in Texas, when a custom van pulled up. An elderly couple got out, and he alternated his conversation between them and me. "The cantaloupes are a dollar each and that's a blessing," he told the couple.

"And how much are the watermelons?" the woman asked.

"Four dollars, and they're fresh out of the fields."

While the lady browsed, he answered one of my questions. "How am I feeling? Some days, I feel forty or fifty, and some days I feel, well, more like ninety."

The lady had a cantaloupe in her hands and he said, "Yes, ma'am, that's a fine one." Brother Wilcox said. "You say you want that watermelon, too? Now, that is a blessing." As he carried the thirty-pound melon to the van, he said, "It's also a blessing that I'm able to carry this for you." Everyone laughed.

As he ambled back from the van, he saw me looking at his shoes. "These shoes may be ugly, but they sure do feel good to my old feet," he said. "They're a blessing, too."

A few minutes later, I was driving toward Macon and I couldn't help but marvel at what a blessing I'd just left behind.

Jazzbo
The Ultimate Entrepreneur
(from columns published in 1990 and 1991)

COCHRAN—Jazzbo, the entrepreneur, is back in business. That bit of news may not mean much if you live in Eatonton or Butler or Hazlehurst. But in Cochran, it means that a downtown fixture has returned, that free enterprise—and, indeed, the American way—is working again.

A raging fire, the second to wipe out a Jazzbo variety store in ten years, put him out of business in 1990, but at age seventy-nine, he started all over again . . . one more time.

Jazzbo's real name is Marion Blanton Weatherly, and he's been a main street merchant (or in the case of Cochran, a Second Street merchant) since 1927, when young Marion hit the road at age sixteen to sell Watkins Products. But he wasn't an ordinary traveling salesperson. He was a snazzy dresser, pointed bow-tie and all. Someone said he was "a jazzy boy." That was soon shortened to just plain—or maybe not so plain—Jazzbo.

In 1942, after he'd married Clara Thompson of Cordele and little Weatherlys began arriving, he opened his first business on Cochran's main drag—a variety store that offered everything from cigarettes to guitar strings. Jazzbo stayed open long hours back when the sidewalks were rolled up and taken in at dark. Effectively, he was a convenience store before convenience stores had sprouted on every corner. He operated by this creed: "Get things other stores don't have, keep prices down and always treat the customer right."

By doing that, he built a loyal following that some merchants only dream about. So, when his first store burned on July 4,

1980, a small army of Jazzbo's customers urged him to make a comeback, even though the fire had cost him an inventory with a worth he estimated at $75,000.

He moved a block up the street and opened another Jazzbo's in a building that had once been a grocery store. Again, he stayed open long hours and treated the customer right. And he prospered.

The latest fire struck on the afternoon of December 6, destroying Jazzbo's and Allied Department Store and forcing a dress shop to move out. Jazzbo, who'd suffered a heart attack and spent a week in the hospital shortly before the fire, was hauled away in an ambulance, suffering from chest pains.

After spending two nights in the hospital, Jazzbo showed up at the fire scene the day after he was released. "I saw him over there talking to people who gathered around," said County Commissioner Jackie Holder. "It looked like he was giving tours of the place."

Jazzbo didn't waste any time looking around for a new place to set up business. And my phone started ringing Monday with a message: "Jazzbo is back in business." His new location at 212 Beech St. is a block and a half away from the old location. But that's a side street in Cochran, and for the first time in forty-eight years, Jazzbo is not on the town's main street. But that isn't his biggest problem.

He's going to have to round up some counters and show-cases. By Tuesday morning, he was selling cigarettes and candy bars straight from the cartons. His only fixtures were a small kitchen table, a cabinet about the size of a nightstand and a grimy little showcase he pulled from the rubble at the old store after he got out of the hospital. His new place also needs new paint. The old tenant, a dress shop, favored pink walls. But in the meantime, store stock is being delivered and the new store—less than half the size of the other one—will be in full operation by this weekend, Jazzbo said. And now that the crisis has eased somewhat, an old story about Jazzbo is being revived and I thought you might like to hear it.

When Jazzbo suffered that first heart attack, he supposedly woke up in the hospital, gazed at the circle of worried faces around his bed, counted heads, and then asked, "Who's minding the store?" I'm not sure that story is true, but right now, Jazzbo is minding the store and maybe that will help things get back to normal in Cochran.

(Jazzbo, invincible as an entrepreneur, lost a battle to cancer and died on January 11, 1993.)

"Hillbilly" Lavender
A Country Boy Can Survive
(from a column published in 1995)

IVEY—A country boy will survive—and thrive—in Ivey, Georgia. Carlton Lavender is living proof. Carlton, also known as "Hillbilly" or "Butterbean," plays a guitar made from a washboard, drives an old pickup truck that's been restored, and is still in love with his first wife. He's got hunting dogs named Shotgun, Buckshot, and Shortshot, and he has a wonderful place to hunt squirrel, rabbit and deer. Besides all that, he wears overalls everywhere except to church.

An unbalanced federal budget isn't going to change Carlton's world. Neither is the war in Bosnia. Or the war on drugs. Drugs? They don't have a place in Carlton's world. Booze, either. He says proudly, "I ain't never set foot in a barroom." Yes, sir, just when I thought this world was running out of characters, along comes Carlton Lavender.

An only child, he was born sixty-one years ago "in a sawmill shack about a mile up Beaver Creek from Ivey Station," he says. His daddy was a farmer, and, by the time Carlton was twelve, he says he was "a full plow hand." If he wanted spending money in those early years, he made that with a plow, too, he said, by plowing other people's fields after he'd finished his chores at home.

When Carlton was fourteen, he started playing a guitar, and he soon became known as "Hillbilly." He certainly sounded the part—and still does. First time you hear him speak, you know he came from far back in the county and has no desire to go uptown with his speech. A little ribbing about that doesn't faze

Carlton. "I live so far back in the boondocks that we don't get the Grand Ole Opry until Tuesday," he says.

By the time he was old enough to go out on his own, he was a natural for the stage. He could play and sing and joke around with the best of them. Everyone loved his countrified, Southern drawl. Family members urged him to go to Nashville and market his talents. But he wouldn't do that. He knew he'd have to play in dives and roadhouses, he said, and that's when he told me that he'd never been in a bar.

Instead, he married Dorothy Sue "Suzie" Carr, also of Ivey, when he was nineteen and she was eighteen. Carlton went to work in the nearby kaolin mines, and they built a house next door to her parents' house. Carlton and Suzie have been right there ever since. They brought up their two children in as peaceful a world as you'll find anywhere.

The only thing wild about the Lavenders' lifestyle was some of Carlton's antics. Like building that guitar from a washboard or wearing long johns over his head and looking through the flap while he performed.

Around home, he's always busy. He uses his farming knowledge to plant a four-acre garden behind his house. Near the home place, he plants a few acres of corn each year "so the people from church can come and get what they want." Pear trees in the back yard furnish the fruit for Suzie's specialty—pear relish. Carlton also grows some sugar cane, and because he does, he also built a grinder on an old farm wagon. But he doesn't have a mule to pull it. That gave way years ago to using a riding lawn mower to turn the grinder.

Strange that he doesn't have a mule. Seems like Carlton has held on to just about everything else. For instance, when a pot will no longer hold water to boil peanuts or cook cane syrup, it becomes a flower pot in the front yard.

And, looking through the woods behind his house, one might conclude that Carlton never traded a truck or automobile. But it turns out that most of those are true antiques—a 1946 Ford farm truck, a 1952 Studebaker pickup, a 1954 Plymouth sedan and a 1974 VW bug. Those, he says, are projects just waiting for the day he retires from the chalk mines. But one project wouldn't wait—his daddy's 1965 Chevy pickup. The elder Lavender died in 1971, but his pickup still sits under a shed in the back yard.

In September 1994, something happened that spurred Carlton into action. His granddaughter, Jennifer, "just about fell through the (hardwood) floorboards (in the bed of the truck)," he said. "So I decided to fix it up." He needed to do that, he said, because the pickup will belong someday to his grandson, Jason.

In the past year, he has—with some professional help—completely reworked the truck, painted it baby blue, and turned it into an eye-catcher around Wilkinson County. Next, he says he will resurrect his mother's 1964 Chevy II, which will belong one day to Jennifer.

Between projects like that and trying to keep up with a full-time job, Carlton, the country boy, still gets calls to perform. Georgia's musicians haven't forgotten that he was one of the original band members at Swampland Opera when it opened twenty years ago. Or that he was once a member of the old Shed House (be careful how you say that) Band that was a fixture for years at the Hiawassee Music Festival in North Georgia.

And, with all that, a country boy can survive.

6

CENTENARIANS: THEY WANT NOTHING BUT YOUR TIME

S*eems like someone is always asking me to explain my fascination with the older generation. Truth is, I never really knew any old folks until I came to Georgia. My last grandparent died when I was just a few weeks old, and because I spent twenty years of my life—from eighteen to thirty-eight—in the Marine Corps, I thought first sergeants and colonels, most of whom were in their forties, were "old folks."*

Soon after I started traveling the back roads of Middle Georgia to write stories. I visited a nursing home for the first time, and something wonderful happened. In all my younger years, I never fell instantly in love with a woman (it took months for me to know that I actually loved Marvalene). But I fell in love with a entire generation that day. And my feelings were especially strong for those over 100 years old.

Old folks, I soon learned, are the most trustworthy generation on the planet. They didn't want to beat me out of anything—not my job, my wallet, my car, or my wife. They just wanted a little bit of my time. And I tried very hard to give it to them. They lived in a time that was so different from ours. But we need to understand their past. Without that, how are we to find our future?

On Living Longer . . .
Like 100 Years or More

Early in my writing career, it seemed only natural to inter-view the few people I could find who had lived to age 100, usually one or two stories a year. In my first ten years with the *Telegraph*, I wrote about less than two dozen. They were memorable people. They were good people. They were interest-ing people. As a result, I can honestly say I've never met a centenarian that I didn't like. But there seemed to be so few of them. . . .

In 1977, I knew just one person over 100. Eli Branch of Soperton was still "dropping seeds" and cultivating a garden with a hand plow at age 102. We lost Mr. Branch at age 103, and by 1979, I still knew just one centenarian—L. A. Whipple of Cochran, the dean of Georgia lawyers who practiced law into his ninety-seventh year and lived to within a few days of his 101st birthday. By 1982, I still had just one friend over 100—Cleo Roberts of Hawkinsville, official grandmother of the Atlanta Braves and a true love in my life until her death at age 101.

However, Middle Georgians who lived past 100 became so numerous in succeeding years that I couldn't get around to writing about all of them. Certainly, I could see this older population growing. In 1984, the 75-and-Over Happy Birthday Club (which still is published each Sunday in the *Telegraph*) listed just seven people over 100. By 1987, they numbered 26, including five birthdays in a single month. In recent years, as many as four people over 100 showed up for the annual Over-75 Party at the Macon Coliseum.

The growing number of centenarians is part of a national trend, I'm told, but even I was surprised by figures listed in a report by the U.S. Census Bureau:

- When the 1980 census was taken, only about 15,000 Americans had reached their 100th birthday.

- By 1985, an estimated 25, 000 had reached 100.

- By 1990, the figure passed the 38,000 mark.

- By the turn of the century, the number is certain to top 100,000.

The Census Bureau offers no concrete explanation for this sudden explosion in the over-100 population, saying that only in the past few years have there been enough people in this age group that a comprehensive study could be conducted to try to determine why people are living so long. Census people ought to talk to the old folks. They offered me some interesting insights on how to live to 100. Listen:

The irrepressible Cleo Roberts said, "Honey, you just live to ninety-nine and then be real careful."

L. A. Whipple, who always seemed amazed that 100 years could pass so quickly, told me, "You've gotta watch out for the traffic. My wife worries that I'll get run over while crossing the street."

Eli Branch said turning somersaults was the best way to celebrate a birthday. And he did it on his 100th.

Of course, the Census Bureau study put things a little differently. It said people over 100 usually list three reasons for long life: orderliness in their lives, growing up in rural areas, and strong religious convictions. I went along with those premises until one day. . . .

The guy in the nursing home obviously was near his end. His hair was as white as snow and his pace was slow. With the aid of a walking cane, he barely got around. He stood propping himself on his cane as I talked to him. "You look like you've certainly traveled many miles down life's road, old timer. To what do you attribute your longevity?"

"First off," he said, "I smoked three packs of cigarettes and a couple of Cuban cigars every day from the time I was maybe fifteen."

Shocked, I said, "You did?"

"Sure did. And I drank, and I caroused, and I did exactly what I wanted to do. Never denied myself anything."

"You did?"

"Sure did."

"Then tell me, how old are you?"

He squinched up his watery eyes and said, "If I see September 7, I'll be forty-two."

Well, I've already done better than that, and, if I follow the advice of my other older friends, perhaps I will live to 100, too.

Nettie Hanson
"On a Bad Day, I Feel like I'm 100"
(from a column published November 24, 1995)

She was born when there were just forty-four of these United States. She was five years old when Babe Ruth was born, and she lived forty-seven years after his death. She was a school-girl when Orville and Wilbur Wright flew the first airplane. She has lived during the times of Geronimo, Mark Twain, and Thomas Edison. She is older than automobiles, moving-picture shows, and professional football. She has lived under the administrations of twenty presidents.

Nettie Medlock Hanson turned 105 in 1995, and she said a couple of days before her birthday that she just might vacuum her apartment—with a Hoover vacuum cleaner that goes back further than, well, the Hoover administration. She was a remarkable woman blessed with amazingly good health. . . .

Born Nettie Medlock in Clayton County on November 24, 1890, she was the oldest of nine children. Nettie spent her early years helping her mama around the house on the family farm. Along the way she often brushed elbows with history. She grew up hearing firsthand accounts about the Civil War from her uncles and grandfather. (Her grandfather was once a guard at Andersonville Prison.) In 1914, she married Leon Hanson and moved to Atlanta. While there, she heard more firsthand stories, this time about Sherman's devastating march through Atlanta.

She also remembers the controversy surrounding the lynching of Leo Frank, the manager of a pencil factory who was convicted of killing thirteen-year-old Mary Phagan. After Frank was taken from the state prison—then in Milledgeville—in

1915 and hanged near Marietta, a chanting mob demanded to see the body on Atlanta streets not far from the Hanson home. (Incidently, Frank, whose death sentence had been commuted by the governor in 1914 to life in prison, was given a pardon by the state in 1986 because he "was deprived of a chance to prove his innocence.")

Later, Nettie took more than a passing interest in Margaret Mitchell's classic novel, "Gone With The Wind." You may recall that the book, which was supposed to be fiction, was based on the lives of real people in Clayton County. Nettie knew some of the O'Haras and the Fitzgeralds in her childhood.

In 1916, the Hansons settled in Macon, and their first and only child, now Hazel Hanson Pittman of Macon, was born here in 1917. Nettie lived a quiet and happy life in our town, and she maintained one of the most beautifully landscaped homes. The multitude of flowers in her yard was planted and pampered by her own hands and ingenuity.

She had interests outside her home, however. Her husband died in 1953, and Nettie went to work as a cashier at Lanier High School at age sixty. For twenty-five years, she *walked* more than a mile to and from the school each day. One reason was that she never learned to drive and didn't want to inconvenience others by asking for a ride.

Nettie didn't move into a retirement home until she passed her eighty-fifth birthday. When she moved, she took her green thumb to Vineville Christian Towers. She planted more flowers, and she was still growing them when I met her shortly after her ninety-ninth birthday.

Jerry Mills, the manager of the high-rise for the elderly, remembers watching storm clouds rolling in and rain beginning to fall. "I went out there and told her she ought to come inside,"

Jerry recalled. "But she said, 'I won't melt.' And she kept on working."

Hazel remembers getting calls about her mother working in the flowers in extreme heat. "But I'd tell them, 'She's happy out there. Leave her alone.' I knew she would come in when she was ready . . . and not before."

The only thing that has slowed down Nettie is a hearing loss. But the only drawback to that, Hazel says, is that her mother doesn't have as much fun at parties as she used to.

Even so, Miss Nettie attended the Over-75 Party at 104, and I remember that Senator Sam Nunn was quite surprised when this Southern lady *walked* onto the dance floor and helped him cut the cake. She was the oldest person ever to attend the party, but, by then, she was accustomed to being the oldest person wherever she went.

Even at age 105, Miss Nettie still patrolled the hallways of Vineville Christian Towers and visited with friends. She could still thread a needle—without eyeglasses—and I guarantee that she read what I wrote about her, too.

She took no daily medication at that age, and she used a cane only occasionally. But did she have any bad days? She smiled and said, "On a bad day, I feel like I'm 100."

Reba Gates
Rolling in the Dough at Age 102
(from a column published on November 6, 1994)

Reba Gates is really rolling in the dough these days—both the mushy stuff and the green stuff. When residents at Magnolia Manor, a retirees' complex in Macon, decided to raise funds to buy a community bus, Mrs. Gates offered to do her share. And she certainly has done that. In just a couple of months, she has rolled enough baker's dough to bring in $265 at a buck a loaf for her special brand of bread. Hmmmm, better make that $266. I bought a loaf, too, and I was munching on it before I got out of the driveway. I can't tell you how good. . . .

Excuse me, back to Mrs. Gates. What makes her different from the others in this fundraising effort is that *she will be 102* next month. That's no typographical error, folks. I said this remarkable lady is still baking at age 102—doing it well and doing it often.

Let me tell you about her and the project she shares with her neighbors. She was born Reba Jones in Macon on December 11, 1892. Her father, Arthur Jones, was a wholesale grocer who made a good living, and young Reba didn't have to do much cooking or baking in her childhood. "We had a cook back then," Mrs. Gates recalled, "and, when I was coming along, the cook ran the kitchen. She didn't want me in the kitchen messing things up."

By the time she was twenty, she was a sophomore at Brenau College in Gainesville, and she decided to marry a dentist named Dr. Paul Gates. "After I got married," she said, "I could cook all I wanted. And I did plenty of it because I wanted Dr. Gates to be happy." She learned a lot of cooking lessons along the way, and she especially became known for her bread, cakes, brownies, and candy. But, you name it, she can make it.

Succeeding generations (Mrs. Gates has two grandchildren and four great-grandchildren) grew up knowing that Grandma could bake up a storm. With a happy laugh, Mrs. Gates admits that, "When I get 'em baked, the children are here to get 'em." As the years began to take a toll on the Gateses, they moved into the Massee Apartments on College Street. Of course, residents there knew she could bake, too.

Dr. Gates died twelve years ago, and it wasn't long before Mrs. Gates heard about a new highrise for the elderly. She became one of the charter residents at Magnolia Manor. Needless to say, it didn't take long for her reputation as a baker to spread among her new neighbors. They virtually stood in line to buy her home-baked bread.

Now let me tell you about the project.

A residents council was formed in September, and the hottest topic right away was the purchase of a bus. "(Magnolia Manor) has a van," said Ann Snow, president of the residents council. "But we need a bus. We'd like to take some trips. And there's another reason. About half of our residents are over eighty years old and many of them don't drive. To meet their needs, we need a bus. So we decided to raise money to buy a twenty-nine-seater."

How much does such a bus cost?

"Between $42,000 and $45,000," Ann said.

"Hey, that's a lot of, uh, dough."

"Well, the residents got busy. They held a yard sale, a bake sale, a car wash—I can't see these folks washing cars, but they said they did it—and bingo games to raise money. And it was only fitting that Mrs. Gates should be a part of it."

"How much have they raised in two months?"

"About $4,800," Ann said, "and that's not bad. We might get some matching funds, you know. But there's more to it than just raising funds," she added. "It's nice just to have plans like this to work toward. There is a lot of enthusiasm for this (fundraiser). I just can't sit still when I think about what we're doing. It's great therapy, too. It makes us forget about our aches and pains."

And they produce some goodies—like Mrs. Gates's bread—that the younger generations really ought to try. As I munched from my loaf the other day, I thought about Mama and that sweet aroma of fresh-baked bread that you could smell from fifty rows deep in a cornfield. . . .

Keep baking, Mrs. Gates. I'll be back. That bus is as good as yours.

Ossie Cook
His Wheels Keep Spinning Even at 100
(from a column that was published on October 9, 1994)

SPARTA—Ossie Cook is an optimist. When he was ninety-four, he bought a new pickup truck. And he financed it. Which tells me that there surely is at least one more optimist somewhere—the banker who took his note. Mr. Cook's optimism, however, was well-founded. He drove that pickup until he was ninety-eight. It still looks shiny new as it sits in his yard.

On October 15, Ossie Cook, the optimist, will turn 100. And, although he doesn't drive anymore "because I don't see too well and I might be bumping into things," he still lives alone. There's a streak of independence in this man that is seldom matched. He certainly gives hope to people like me. I can't tell you how good it feels to talk to someone who's *more than forty years* older than I am.

Mr. Cook was born on October 15, 1894, in a little log house in Washington County that's only about thirteen miles from where he now resides. He was the second of thirteen children. (Five of his siblings are still alive—Woodrow Cook, 80, of Hancock County; Clemmie Dixon, 86, of Forsyth; and Ada Smith, 97, Ruth Martin, 88, and Margaret Ivester, 77, all of Milledgeville.) Ossie, the first-born, usually had the chore of going after the doctor as Cook children were born.

Young Ossie joined the Army in July 1918, sailed across the Atlantic in a captured German vessel, and arrived in Europe just in time to be pressed into the battle of the Argonne Forest. By Armistice Day, his quartermaster unit of the 83rd Division reached the Rhine River. But before Ossie had time to celebrate, he came down with the mumps and spent Christmas in a "mumps ward" in LeMans, France. "Santa Claus came to see us," he said, "and he brought me some peppermint candy, but, with the mumps I couldn't eat it."

After kicking the mumps, he spent six months helping clear land and building an American military camp near Le Mans. Then he was released from the Army and returned to Hancock County.

He tried farming for a while, he said, "but the boll weevil ate us up in 1921." So he moved from Washington County to the land where he now lives, did a little farming and worked in a sawmill for a couple of years. In 1924, he married Mary Glynn Anderson, and for several years he did whatever job he had to do to make a living. He drove a lumber truck, farmed, worked in the sawmill.

In 1926, he became a salesman for Singer Sewing Machine company, and he sold the first electric sewing machine in Hancock County to Elizabeth Stewart that year. In ensuing years, he said, "I sold a heap of those things." Then he paused and his sharp-as-a-tack memory took him back. "Well, I didn't sell a whole lot during the Hoover days (the Great Depression), but neither did anyone else."

Of course, times got better, and he and Mary Glynn reared seven children on what he could make selling sewing machines and what they could make together on the farm.

Mr. Cook never got wealthy, but he got comfortable. As the years passed, he amazed his family and friends with his get-up-and-go. His neat little home five miles outside Sparta became a gathering place for his seven children, twenty grandchildren, twenty-eight great-grandchildren, and two great-greats. And they learned a great deal at Grandpa's knee. "Be honest," he told them. "Go to church. Learn all you can. Take care of yourselves (physically)—no drinking, no drugs."

Mr. Cook heeded his own advice, and also set an example in loyalty and dedication. For instance, Mary Glynn died in 1943, but he never married again. When I asked why, he said simply, "My children needed my attention."

And he must have taken very good care of himself. He takes only vitamins, no prescription medicine, says his daughter, Sadie Boyer.

On the other hand, his eyesight is now too poor to drive (if indeed the state would issue a driver's license to anyone 100 years old) and he has experienced unsteadiness on his feet at times. In fact, he went from a cane to a walker after a fall in 1992. But he insists that he's not all used up. "If I lie down in a nursing home," he said, "I'll die for sure. I can still work these," he said, kicking his legs vigorously, "so there's no reason to just sit . . . and do nothing."

So he pays a young lady, Linda Davis, to come to his house each morning, help him get dressed, cook his breakfast, and take him where he wants to go in that truck in the yard. Three daughters live within a few minutes' drive, and they alternately take care of his few other needs—like evening meals and baths. In the evenings, he watches TV—usually alone—and tries "not to crumble away too much" before Linda comes back the next morning.

On Sundays, he can be found at Zebulon Methodist Church in Hancock County. That's where he joined family members, friends and fellow parishioners to celebrate birthday No. 100.

Hennie Lou Palmer
"In a Land Where We'll Never Grow Old"
(from a column published on October 3, 1993)

GLENWOOD—Something unusual happened the other day. A lady serenaded Ol' Boyd with an old song. It was unusual for a couple of reasons. First, I don't get serenaded very often. And second, the lady doing the singing was old enough to be my *grandmother*. Think about it and do a little arithmetic, and you'll probably guess that my serenader was around 100.

Remarkable, you say? Yes, Hennie Lou Palmer is very remarkable. She will turn 105 in a few days, and she's still singing. Is she sharp? For sure. When I asked when she got married, she said, "A few months before my twentieth birthday—on the 16th of July in 1908." Do a little more arithmetic, dear reader, and you'll see what I mean about being sharp.

She was born Hennie Lou Johnson in Macon County on October 9, 1888, and her age is not a matter for debate. Not only does she have the family Bible to prove her age, but she has a son, Lewis Palmer of Mount Vernon, who is going to turn eighty-four two days after his mom's 105th birthday.

Young Hennie Lou grew up on the farm, and her daddy surely was one versatile farmer. He grew corn, pulled it, stored it, shelled it, ground it into meal and hauled it to market.

Young Hennie Lou went to school through the eighth grade—which is all there was in Macon County at the time.

In 1907, she met Claybourn Palmer, a Wheeler County native, who was working as a bookkeeper for King Lumber and Oil Company in Unadilla.

They courted in a horse and buggy "for a year and a day," she said. And just to give you an idea of the period of time we're talking about, young Hennie Lou didn't see an automobile until she was eighteen years old, and she didn't ride in a car until after she was married.

After about fifteen years in Unadilla, the family—which by then included two sons, Lewis and Oakley—moved to Wheeler County. "We came here to farm cotton," Mrs. Palmer said, "but it was the most miserable five years of my life." Indeed, the boll weevil invaded their fields and the Palmers "went flat broke and lost it all," Lewis Palmer recalled.

But Claybourn Palmer knew how to make a comeback. He established a store in Mount Vernon and then got into buying and selling livestock. The Palmer family also ran the town's ice house for many years, moving up to forty of those 300-pound blocks of ice a day—"until refrigerators put us out of that business," Lewis said.

Mrs. Palmer was always a homemaker, and she was "a great cook," according to Lewis's wife, Sadie. Mrs. Palmer, a dedicated flower grower, also was active in the Mount Vernon Garden Club for more years than anyone can remember.

I hope that she won't mind me calling her a homebody. After all, she never traveled far, preferring to stay close to home and sleep in her own bed at night. She once traveled as far as Memphis, but in 105 years, she has never stepped into an airplane, she said.

Mrs. Palmer was very close to her husband, who died in 1974 at age eighty-nine. But her life has included one other remarkable relationship. Lewis and Sadie were married in 1939, and for all of the years since, the two couples shared a home. "When we first got married," Sadie said, "we lived with them. And later, they lived with us. We've always been together."

With their good care, Mrs. Palmer lived at home past her 100th birthday. She could still get around pretty well until she fell four years ago, breaking a hip and her left arm. After she recovered, she preferred to keep her hospital room, and for four years, she has been a resident of Wheeler County Hospital. If she was moved into a nursing home, Medicare would "pay every dime," Lewis said. But they want Mrs. Palmer to have the very best care, so they pay the tab for her to have it.

Her room is still decorated with last year's birthday greetings, including one with a huge "104" on it. I was admiring those decorations when she asked if she could sing a song for me. She launched into a good old Baptist hymn, "In a Land Where We'll Never Grow Old." And she's pretty good, folks. A couple of nurses stopped at the door to listen and then applauded when she'd finished.

Back at the office, I learned something about the song Mrs. Palmer had sung to me. It was copyrighted in 1930 by Jasper C. Moore, a graduate of Mercer University who spent his adult life preaching in South Georgia churches.

And there's one bit of irony here. My songstress and the songwriter were born in the same year—1888. Brother Moore died in 1962.

Alfred Fambro
"Mayor of Lamar Road"

Folks along Lamar Road in Macon don't bother to hold elections. But you can ask anyone out there who the mayor is, and you'll get directions to Alfred Fambro's house. Yes, everyone knows "the mayor of Lamar Road." And he knows everybody who lives in the dozen homes along the country road in northern Bibb County. He has either known them since they were born, or he can tell you when they moved in because he welcomed every one of them personally.

Mr. Fambro is just the kind of mayor everyone would like to have. He knows who is sick, widowed or disabled. If a resident's mobility is impaired in any way, you can bet that the mayor will come hiking up the way on trash day and push the green monsters to the roadway. He does countless little chores and favors that endear him to others and make him a welcome visitor in any household.

If you think he isn't the mayor of Lamar Road, tell you what we'll do. Put Alfred Fambro, Mayor David Carter, and Governor Zell Miller on the ballot and see who wins. Mr. Fambro by a landslide. Guaranteed.

What makes me so sure of that? Mr. Fambro got a fifty-year head start on either of those veteran politicians. You see, he'll soon turn 100, and even though he says he's "running on the used-to-be," don't think for a minute that his get-up-and-go has got up and went. This man still splits his own firewood, walks half a mile uphill just to visit, mows his yard and . . . Well, just listen to his story and then I think you would vote for him, too.

Alfred Fambro was born in the Thomaston Road area of Bibb County on November 9, 1899. If you've heard of Fambro

Chapel, then you know his roots run deep. That historic old church was named for his great-uncle, Sam Fambro, who donated the land on which the church is built.

Alfred's father, John Fambro, moved his family to Lamar Road when Alfred was just four years old. That was in 1903, and that's why Mr. Fambro can now recite the history of Lamar Road as though he was reading from a book.

Indeed, this man is blessed with a remarkable memory. He can tell you how and when each parcel of land changed hands. He talks about 1917 or 1922 like it was yesterday. He remembers that he helped his father pay for a forty-acre parcel of land in a manner that would be considered pretty peculiar today. "There wasn't a lot of money (in 1922)," he said. "So we paid two bales of cotton per year on the place until we had it paid for."

To get supplies for their farm, the Fambros would load a mule-drawn wagon with eggs, butter, and chickens, then drive to G. S. Waldorf's Store on Poplar Street in downtown Macon to trade for what they couldn't produce on the farm.

Young Alfred proved to be quite an athlete, too. In 1918, he started playing baseball for the Lorain Stars. (There used to be a community north of Macon called Lorain Station.) I asked if he was pretty good. "The best there was," he said, and he didn't sound like he was bragging. "I played center field, and I was so fast that people called me 'Rabbit.' Yes, sir, I could run."

In 1926, he started doing construction work, and he was soon making $12.50 a week, cash money. With that kind of income and still being single, he bought his first car, a Model-T Ford. "I paid $50 down and $12.50 a month until it was paid for," he recalled, "and there was no carrying charge."

Baseball star. Bachelor with a car. I'll just bet that Alfred Fambro was the talk of Lamar Road in those days.

Even now, a ride along Lamar Road with him is a delight. "See that tree?" he asked, pointing to a shade tree in a neighbor's yard. "My daddy set out that tree in 1923. I've watched it do a lot of growing."

Indeed, he has. And he has seen a lot of other things happen along Lamar Road. When white people began buying land and moving out that way, Alfred Fambro welcomed them and did favors for them just like he'd always done for those already living there. "He's so good to his neighbors," says Mary Standard. "He helps look after them. He's a fine friend."

The mayor smiled and said, "Well, we came up the hard way, didn't we? We had to work to make a living and . . ." He paused and said, "Shoot, I remember when she was born. I was working for her daddy at the time. That would have been about . . . oh, sixty-five years ago."

But to the man with the sharp mind, it fit right in there with another memory. "My grandson, Carl Fambro, was the first black commander of the ROTC at Central High," he said with pride in knowing that this name was revered in other places.

Yes, the years have slipped by, and Alfred Fambro hardly looks any worse for the wear. Is he as healthy as he looks? "Actually," he said, "I've got eye trouble, so I don't drive anymore. And I have an enlarged heart. And I have sugar diabetes."

But he has an answer for advancing age. "I keep moving," he said. "If I sit still too long, I know it would be hard to get moving again." Moving. Up the hill to help a neighbor. Out in the yard to split firewood. In the back yard to plant a garden. The mayor of Lamar Road is indeed on the move.

(As this book goes to press, folks along Lamar Road are planning a big birthday bash to celebrate Mr. Fambro's 100th birthday.)

7

MY HEROES:
SOME GREAT AMERICANS

M y heroes come in many
different sizes, ages, skin colors, and nationalities. And they
are heroes for different reasons—from an immigrant who
worked any kind of job she could find (and then used her
earnings to help others) to a man who rode his daughter's
bicycle thirty-one miles to work, just to try to hold on to a job
he liked; from a mother who made every sacrifice to care for
a mentally challenged son for fifty years to Harry Ullmann,
hero of a real war. These are the stories that kick-started me
in the morning and kept me truly interested—for twenty-five
years—in the job I was doing. Here are my heroes. . . .

Harry Ullmann
Twice a Prisoner of War
(from a column published in 1989)

When I start counting the most patriotic Americans I know, Harry Ullmann of Macon ranks right up there with the best of them. Tell me, how many people do you know who get real tears in their eyes when they hear the "Star Spangled Banner" or "God Bless America"? Harry does. He loves this country and what it stands for as much as anyone I have ever known. Listen to his story and I think you'll understand why.

He was born Helmut Ullmann, the son of a farmer in Hohndorf in what used to be called East Germany. He was a bright kid who finished junior college at age fifteen. Young Helmut read everything he could get his hands on, including novels about America's Old West. He longed to live in the wide open spaces of Texas and become a cowboy. He also wanted the freedoms we enjoy in America and wanted to get away from a war that was destroying his native land.

By 1942, the year that Helmut finished junior college, things were not going well for Adolph Hitler's armies. The Fuhrer was down to drafting sixteen-year-olds and a few weeks before his sixteenth birthday, Helmut was called. Although he was barely old enough to have a driver's license, he became one of the youngest tank drivers in the Panzer divisions. I saw a picture of him at that age. He hadn't even been introduced to a razor.

In the fall of 1944, he was driving a tank in Holland, where German troops were locked in battle with America's elite 82nd Airborne Division, when his tank was knocked out by a bazooka and he was captured. However, he remained a prisoner of war for less than twenty-four hours as German troops retook the area and returned him to his unit.

Six months later, he was captured again, this time by Canadian troops, and he spent nearly four years as a POW, working in France, Holland, Belgium, England, and Scotland. He remembers that the coal mines in Belgium were the worst of it; the picturesque farms of Scotland were the best of it. From afar, he watched as his country became divided. And even though he longed to see his parents, two brothers, and sister, he did not want to live in his old homeland. For a while, that didn't matter since he was still a POW.

On December 29, 1948, he was released, but he still didn't return. "I wanted to go to America right then, but I couldn't get a passport." He showed me several old letters informing him that his requests for a passport had been turned down. While he waited, he decided to see his family one time before going to America. So he went to Germany and simply "walked across the border in broad daylight." He spent a week with his family. It would be the last time he would see his mother alive.

Then, to avoid any disagreement, he told his family he was going back across the border to get his other possessions. But actually, he never intended to return.

At the border, he could not produce a passport. So he was arrested and thrown into a cellar. For three days and nights, he was interrogated. On the fourth night he escaped. After so many years, he still doesn't discuss details of that escape.

But he made it back to England and started pestering the U.S. consul's office once again about a passport. In January 1950, the passport came through. He still has a copy of the want ad where he sold his accordion, bicycle, and other possessions to raise thirty-one English pounds for passage on the Queen Mary.

Upon arrival in New York, he caught a train directly to Houston, Texas, where an aunt lived. But he never became a cowboy. He went to work for Borden's Dairies. Even though he spoke little English, he worked hard and gained promotions. "I didn't have anybody," he recalled, "so I went to work early and left late."

Then Uncle Sam came calling. One year after his arrival in Houston, he got an official letter. He could make out two things—that it came from the president and that it said, "Greetings."

"I was happy. I thought, 'Gee, the president knows I got here OK.' But the women (at the plant) started crying and saying that I was going to have to go bye-bye." Harry was 23 when he was drafted and the Army wanted to send him to Officer's Candidate School. But there was a small problem—Harry was not yet a citizen of the United States.

So he went to Fort Bragg, North Carolina, and trained with (who else?) the 82nd Airborne Division, which had once held him prisoner. He made twenty-odd jumps and might have gone to Korea if he had not seriously injured his back in a jump in 1952. He never jumped again, but he finished his two-year hitch, got his honorable discharge and gained his citizenship in this country in 1954.

But let me back up. While he was in jump school at Fort Benning in 1952, he went on a blind date in nearby LaGrange, met a girl named Joyce and wound up marrying her some months later.

After getting out of the Army, Harry went back to Houston and resumed his job with Borden's Dairies. In 1954, he moved to the Borden's plant in Augusta, and when the new Borden's plant was put in operation in Macon a few months later, he came here. He's been there ever since—except for a few vacations that included seven trips back to Germany to see members of what remain of his family.

Harry and Joyce Ullmann became fixtures in South Macon. They reared two sons—Terry, now a medical doctor, and Tony, an insurance adjuster.

Harry and Joyce made many friends and served in all sorts of volunteer jobs. But they made the deepest impression on the bowling scene. That's where I met them. Joyce is secretary of our bowling league, and Harry . . . well, Harry is the guy all of the women hug every time they see him. (One of these days, I'm going to discover his secret.)

Harry told me the other day that he's planning a trip to Columbus this summer to see some of his old Army buddies. And we talked about being an American. That's when Harry told me about how he can't keep the tears out of his eyes when he hears America's songs.

There aren't many who really cry at times like that. And there aren't many who would admit it. But that's what makes Harry Ullmann a great American.

Gabriela Bardizbanian
A Real American (To Be) Hero
(from a column published on February 23, 1996)

The accent is heavy, but the message is clear when Gabriela Bardizbanian speaks. "In this country, if you want something, you can have it," she says. "All you have to do is work for it. It's not that way where I came from." She came from Bulgaria, a socialist republic in eastern Europe where a person has pretty much what the government wants a person to have.

Those who know Gabriela, who understand a little about her homeland, who know the sacrifices she has made . . . those people stand in awe of her. "In this country, we take everything for granted," says co-worker Jean Lawrence. "Gabriela doesn't. She appreciates the opportunity she was given in this country, and she gives back so much of herself."

How much has she given back? Well, there was a time when she took a job far below her skills level, worked sixteen hours a day and then spent a good bit of her earnings on others. Gabriela gives blood, gives to United Way, gives to the education of others, even gives to the Olympic Committee. Give, give, give. That pretty much sums up the story of this remarkable thirty-year-old woman, but let me give you some of the details.

Gabriela was born and grew up in Plovdiv, the second largest city in a country that is smaller than our state. Her father, a hospital lab technician, raised Gabriela to be a world-class skier. Athletes in her country are highly regarded and supported rather comfortably by the government.

Gabriela started skiing at age three, and she practiced very hard to become a champion. But something else impressed

Gabriela when she was a little girl. She saw the Olympic torch being carried through her hometown and she hoped that one day she would be the kind of athlete who could bear that torch. Before she finished high school, she was winning national water-skiing championships. She kept winning in college, where she majored in physical education. Then she married Stepan Bardizbanian who was winning men's championships with equal consistency, and they started a family.

In December 1989, Gabriela and Stepan came to this country for a Christmas visit with relatives in New York City. At that time, Communist governments were being overthrown, the Iron Curtain came tumbling down, and old lifestyles changed almost overnight. Bulgaria was in turmoil. "We didn't like what was happening," she recalled, "so we decided to stay (in the United States)."

That was an especially hard decision since their infant son, Denny, remained in Bulgaria with his grandparents, and they had no immediate means of bringing him to this country. The Bardizbanians had good contacts in Georgia—Ed and Carol Walker of Milledgeville—who had taken an American skiing team to Bulgaria for international competition several years before, and a friendship had developed. So they came south.

The Walkers already knew what folks in Milledgeville would soon find out—that the Bardizbanians are hard-working, well-educated, compassionate people. With the help of the Walkers, the young couple and their oldest son, Gary, set up housekeeping in Milledgeville. Soon the couple went to work at the Forstmann plant at the edge of Milledgeville.

Gabriela, who spoke no English at the time, took a job as a spinning operator and never complained. She remembers working "sixteen hours a day, seven days a week." But that was not a complaint. She and Stepan wanted to help others with the money they made by working overtime. In the past six years, they have sponsored six international students to come to America, and she and Stepan paid for the tuition of each.

Of course, it didn't take long for the plant's management to recognize the Bardizbanian work ethic. Gabriela is now an administrative plant assistant. Stepan moved to another plant and is now a supervisor at Universal Forest Products, a maker of roof trusses.

I'm sure that you are wondering about things like: How is Gabriela's English now? Good enough that she was accepted as an interpreter when the Russian basketball team was touring this country in 1994-1995. (Stepan also worked as a volunteer interpreter.)

Has Gabriela used her considerable skiing talents in this country? Yes. She volunteers her time with the Georgia College Athletic Department, and she organized and now coaches the GC team that finished second in the national college championships. She also teaches young children to ski, and two of them already have made the news. Ten-year-old Regina Jaques of Atlanta has set several national records in her age group, and Kristine Cotton of Macon made the United States ski team and finished second in World Cup competition.

Whatever happened to little Denny? He came to this country after a five-year separation from his parents, and, even though they worried about his ability to learn English in a very short time and stay on track in school, they shouldn't have. "Two weeks after he started school," Gabriela said, "I got a note from the teacher saying he talks too much."

Will the Bardizbanians become citizens of the United States? They have applied, and, yes, they will become citizens. If they're not accepted, I will personally picket immigration offices.

And, finally, what about that little girl's long-ago dream of carrying the Olympic torch? The folks at Forstmann think so much of Gabriela that the company submitted her name to be a torch bearer for this year's Olympics in Atlanta. She found out a couple of weeks ago that she was indeed chosen.

But this story will not end in July. Gabriela Bardizbanian was put on this earth to help others, and she is not likely to finish that task anytime soon.

Mitchell Holland
A Man with His Own Opus
(from a column published on February 4, 1996)

COCHRAN— Mr. Holland loved music. He taught high school students how to play and how to march in a band. Mr. Holland was also a fine musician in his own right, and he performed with big bands and orchestras from time to time. He and his wife had one child who was born deaf. Mr. Holland had to make great sacrifices to see that his son got an education and became a productive member of society.

By now, you're saying, "Aw, you saw that movie, too. I didn't know you did movie reviews."

This isn't a movie review, dear reader. This is real life. The Mr. Holland I'm talking about lives in Cochran, Georgia, and Mitchell Holland Sr. had no idea that the movie, "Mr. Holland's Opus," so closely resembled his own story until I told him about it.

But now he wonders—and so do I—about a most remarkable coincidence. . . .

Mitchell Holland was born in Cochran seventy-four years ago. His family moved to Crawfordville when he was two, and he finished high school there. Then he moved back to Cochran to study music at Middle Georgia College.

Unlike the movie's Glen Holland (played by Richard Dreyfus) who taught high school music to allow him time to finish his great musical composition, Mitchell Holland would have been perfectly happy with the thirty-year career in high school music that the movie's Mr. Holland enjoyed. Mitchell Holland was a pioneer in high school music in this area. He formed the first marching band at Eastman High in 1949, and he did it the hard way. "Band directors were not certified (teachers) in those days," he recalled, "and if a band director was going to get paid, the money had to come from the parents. Schools paid nothing."

For five years, he directed the band in Eastman. However, when a new superintendent came into office, things changed. "He told me that he didn't care whether we had a band or not," Mr. Holland said. So he moved on—to his hometown—and started a high school marching band at Cochran High.

"But the money was never here like it was in Eastman," he said. "Rich people there—the Stuckeys and the Mullises and others—backed me up pretty well for a while. In Cochran, I had to run for the school board (and win) just to get a bond issue floated to build a band room onto the gymnasium."

He was a pioneer in another area. He lobbied state officials to certify band directors so they could be paid like other teachers. (That's why band directors throughout this state owe this man, and they owe him big time.)

Just when he started seeing some progress on those fronts, the real-life Mr. Holland had to rethink his priorities. Mitchell Holland Jr. was born deaf because of a lack of oxygen at birth. He would need a lot of help to succeed in life.

Unlike the movie's Mr. Holland, who didn't want to be distracted from writing his great piece of music to spend time with his son, little Mitch's future became our Mr. Holland's obsession. He gave up the field of endeavor he loved so much, and he quit journeying around the country to play with the likes of the Glenn Miller Band. He opened an insurance agency to earn enough to pay for "more than one hundred trips to Atlanta and Florida" to see audiology specialists. All the time, little Mitch was solving the problem himself. He became perhaps the best lip reader in the world.

While the celluloid Mr. Holland was struggling to pay for his son's special schools and training in sign language, the real-life son relied solely on lip reading. And, while the son in the movie went to schools for the deaf, Mitch moved into the mainstream.

But don't think Mitch just barely got through school. He excelled. He was an honors student at Cochran High, and when he graduated, he didn't rest on that accomplishment.

Mitch went to Middle Georgia and the University of Georgia and Georgia College. The further he went, the more difficult his studies became. College professors weren't as understanding or as helpful as his high school teachers had been, Mitch recalled. But he persevered, his father said. "I remember Mitch sitting at that (dining room) table late into the night, night after night," Mr. Holland said. "He'd have ten or twelve books piled up there, and he would study and study and study."

His mother was young Mitch's inspiration, he told me the other day. Mr. Holland, too, gives his wife credit for much of his son's achievements. "I had to get out and make a living," he said, "and I worked some very long hours. But she was right there with him, helping him, encouraging him."

Evelyn Mitchell, a severe diabetic, died in 1985, but not before she saw her son walk in two college graduation lines—once for a bachelor's degree and again for a master's degree. She also saw him go to work as media specialist at Jeffersonville Elementary School, a job he now has held for twenty-four years.

Mr. Holland, the once energetic band leader, was stricken by rheumatoid arthritis some years ago. His body is disfigured by the disease, and he can hardly get around.

His son, who never married, lives with him in the neat little home on East Dykes Street in Cochran, and Mitch now takes care of his father as his father once took care of him.

And they obviously have a deep admiration for one another. "I don't really know how Mitch accomplished all that he has," Mr. Holland said, "but he has done things I'm sure I never could have done."

Mitch shrugged and said, "I had a lot of encouragement at home. It never occurred to me that I couldn't do it."

I would say that Mr. Holland's life would make a great movie, but who would go to see two movies so much alike?

Still, I'm glad I had the chance to tell you about the real Mr. Holland.

Jane Perry
A Woman of Note
(from a column published on December 4, 1994)

WARNER ROBINS—I could only watch in utter fascination as her fingers glided skillfully across the piano keys, extracting a world-class rendition of "Fantasia Impromptu" from the classroom piano. Extraordinary sounds from an ordinary piano. It was indeed a plain sort of instrument, much like the one on which I once tried to learn to play "Chopsticks." It certainly wasn't one of those fancy, expensive, oh-so-carefully tuned concert pianos.

And the woman playing the piano? Her name is Jane Perry. She is deaf—very nearly stone deaf. With the help of hearing aids, she can hear thunder and middle-range musical notes. She can hear your voice, but cannot distinguish the words you are saying.

She lost her hearing to childhood illnesses, but then she was blessed with a rare gift—something known in musical circles as "perfect pitch."

Given this much, Jane chose not to be held captive in a soundless world, but to use her minute amount of hearing—and that gift of perfect pitch—to become a music teacher *and* a concert pianist. And a warm, vibrant human being who could lead a full life. Jane Perry is truly one of the most amazing people I've ever met.

She was born Jane Stuckenbruck, and she grew up in southern Germany where her parents were American missionaries for the Christian Church (Disciples of Christ). Her family enjoyed a rich tradition in music. She can trace her musical roots back several generations. All three of her brothers are gifted musicians, including violinist Dr. Dale Stuckenbruck of New York City. He plays for Broadway shows in the Big Apple, performs in concerts, and plays with the Brooklyn Symphony.

But back to Jane. She was stricken with several illnesses when she was still an infant, including high fever and measles. She was treated with streptomycin, which doctors later blamed for her hearing loss.

Neither she nor her parents knew sign language, but they managed to communicate with Jane through gestures and expressions. When Jane was six, she got her first hearing aid and heard her first musical notes. On her seventh birthday, Jane's father had a piano delivered to their house in Tübingen, a town about fifteen miles south of Stuttgart. "I thought it was a game," she said. "I'd hit the keys, but nothing happened." Shortly afterward, something did happen. She took piano lessons from Rolf Sturm, a well-known German pianist. And the lessons weren't wasted.

Jane loved music, and she would practice up to eight hours a day. "I loved to practice," she said, "and I still do." When she was just thirteen, Jane played her first concerto for the public, and when she was fourteen, she wrote an opera. Through it all, she never let her hearing problems be a problem. "I didn't meet another deaf person until I was twenty years old," she said.

Her lack of communication skills was a challenge, she said. "I went to the first grade three times—first to a German school, then to a school on an (American) Army base, then to a semi-private German school." It ultimately became necessary that her parents do most of the teaching at home. And they surely did a wonderful job.

When Jane was twenty, she returned to the United States and entered the North Carolina School of Arts in Winston-Salem. Four years later, she graduated with a degree in music and added a master's degree in 1977. That same year, Jane Stuckenbruck met and married Bob Perry, now a fifth-grade teacher at Tucker Elementary School in Perry. Since their marriage, Bob has earned two master's degrees, both having to do with teaching the hearing impaired.

Bob is also "a wonderful singer," his wife says. But then Jane added as her face turned red: "I don't pronounce some of my words too well, and I once said I was married to a wonderful *sinner*." But don't let her kid you about her words. For someone who can't hear what she is saying, she speaks extremely well.

The Perrys moved to Georgia in 1987 when Bob was hired to teach the hearing impaired in Houston County schools. Of course, Jane started teaching music right away, and she's more of an education than some students expected. You see, every student in her seven classes must learn sign language. (Take my word for it, that's a skill those students will always be happy they have.)

Jane's very existence is built around music. Besides the piano, she can play the accordion, flute and all four recorders (conical wind instruments with whistle mouthpieces). But her forte is piano, and she maintains a studio at home where she teaches—and practices—in the evening.

Music will run in her family for at least one more generation. The only Perry offspring, Angela Grace, age thirteen, already plays the harp for weddings and receptions at the local historical society.

In Jane's classroom at Pearl Stephens Elementary School on the south side of Warner Robins, she teaches music theory and history and how to play the recorders.

Her 1994-95 classes put together a version of "The Nutcracker," and among those who attended were Earl and Ottie

Mearl Stuckenbruck, the parents who helped a deaf child to become a great success story.

Later, I would find out that Jane Perry taught one very special student—E. Z. Cleghorn, a second-grader who is being mainstreamed into the public schools even though he is blind. Mrs. Perry teaches song and dance routines to E. Z. by placing her hands on his head and guiding him through a routine.

Some team, these two.

Felix Gonzalez
Dedicated to His Job
(from a column published on October 7, 1994)

I don't want to put you in an awkward position, but I would like for you to consider a situation and then tell me what you might have done under similar circumstances: You are married with a wife and three children. After years of bouncing from one job to another, you've finally found the kind of work you've always wanted. You're a dental lab technician. Just when you're getting settled into this job, your car won't start one morning. You haven't missed a day of work in eight months on the job, and people there believe in you. What do you do?

A) Call a friend for a ride?
B) Call in sick?
C) Call and simply tell your boss you won't be there?
D) Borrow your daughter's bicycle and start pedaling the 31 miles to your job?

Felix Gonzalez didn't have a telephone, so answer "D" was the obvious choice. No, I'm not kidding. It really happened just a few months ago. Felix did that because he was trying to hold onto a small slice of the American dream—a decent job. And he wasn't willing to let even a balky car take it away from him. Of course, you'll want to hear about his remarkable man, and, of course, I'm going to tell you about him.

Felix was born in Chicago, the first of nine children of a Puerto Rican chef who was working in an Italian restaurant on Chicago's north side. Because Felix was born in this country, he is an American citizen. But his family eventually returned to Puerto Rico, and Felix spent some growing-up years there.

However, his heart always was in this country, and when his father died in 1974, Felix, then eighteen, told his mother that he was returning to the United States. He moved back to Chicago and worked for a while as a chef's assistant in the same restaurant where his father once toiled. But Felix wanted a trade of his own very badly. In 1986, he entered a vocational college to become a dental lab technician. While there, he met and married a lady named Edie, the divorced mother of one child.

Felix was a dedicated student. He finished first in his class, and by the time he graduated, he already had a job. But soon, the work load at his lab declined rapidly. "The work was going to labs where Mexicans—Mexicans without (immigration) papers—worked for two dollars an hour," he said. By 1989, he was out of work and the job market in Chicago was "pitiful," he said. Edie, who grew up in this area, suggested that they try Georgia. So they came South.

At first, Felix worked in construction, but those jobs were iffy at best. Once he even left Georgia, thinking that job prospects might be better in Philadelphia where one of his brothers lived. But his time in Philadelphia certainly made one point quite clear to him—he didn't want to raise his children in a big city. So he came back to Macon.

Felix can tell plenty of stories about trying to raise three children on jobs that always seemed to pay near-minimum wages. It's especially tough since Edie can't work. You see, their youngest child, Kobi, age four, is asthmatic and must go on a breathing machine four times every day.

At one time, he had an old car. It had rusted-out floorboards and a balky engine, but it was transportation until a driver rear-ended Felix's car and police officers discovered that Felix didn't have current insurance. His car was "confiscated," he said.

At times, he sought help from the social services system, he said, "but I was always told that I made too much money" to be eligible for assistance. He was told that, he said, even when his gross pay was $250 per week.

About a year ago, Edie noticed an advertisement in the classified section of this newspaper for a dental lab technician, Felix's chosen field. An old fire was rekindled. Bob Graham, the owner of that lab, gave Felix a tryout, and Felix seemed to have found his niche.

Felix appreciated his co-workers, and he tried to never inconvenience them. For instance, he never asked for a ride, even when he was walking more than four miles each morning to work and four more miles back home each evening. When his co-workers found out, they arranged transportation for him until he was financially able to buy a car. His next set of wheels was a 1983 Chevy station wagon, and it got him to and from work most of the time—even after he moved to Crawford County to rent a bigger place for his family.

He did all right until that morning in June. Since he didn't have a phone, he couldn't call in, he said. He borrowed Jennifer's bike and started pedaling toward Macon. By the time he reached Lizella and found a pay phone, he was ten minutes late for work. He called and told co-worker Wayne McClendon that he was running late because he was riding a bicycle to work.

"We were stunned," said Harriet Wade, manager at Technident. "We said, 'He's riding a *what* to work?' We could hardly believe it, but we decided someone ought to go after him. By the time Wayne got out on Eisenhower Parkway, Felix had reached Sam's Warehouse."

That incident rallied folks to Felix's side. Sherrill Graham, the lab owner's daughter, said she owned a house on Bishop Road and that she was willing to rent it to Felix. On second thought, she said, she was impressed enough with Felix that she would sell the house for no money down and payments of normal rent.

Felix and Edie, along with Jennifer, age thirteen, Christy, age six, and Kobi moved into the first home they have ever owned this past Tuesday night. By Thursday, Felix was surely the happiest man in Macon. "This house is a first step," he said about buying the house. "My wife is thrilled. My children are happy. And this is what I wanted for them. It makes me very happy, too."

The American dream has come true. Again.

Susan Lee
A Drive for Life
(from a column published on October 18, 1992)

FORT VALLEY—Right now, Susan Lee's best hope for survival in a battle with leukemia is that modern medicine will progress very quickly. Every day that passes brings us a little closer to a cure for leukemia, and Susan knows it.

But she isn't just sitting and waiting. Susan, a teacher and a mother of two, knows that the latest—and best—weapon against leukemia is a bone marrow transplant. Because of that, she kicked off a campaign earlier this month to register potential bone marrow donors in Middle Georgia—donors who might mean survival for herself and others. In the four months since her own diagnosis, she has had remarkable success with the drive and she is now working on plans to bring her crusade to Macon in early 1993. Of course, I want you to hear her story and help out if you can.

Susan Jones was born in Perry forty years ago, and she married Fort Valley insurance broker Jack Lee. In June, she went to a doctor to check on what she thought was "a pulled stomach muscle," but a routine blood test showed that she had "an elevated white blood count," which translates to leukemia. "At first, I thought it was a lot more treatable than it really is," she recalled. "But I was told that the only known cure would be a bone marrow transplant.

Doctors at Vanderbilt University Hospital in Nashville, however, told her that it would be a least a year before a transplant would be possible. In the meantime, they prescribed a mild form of chemotherapy in an attempt to control her leukemia. During the next year, they want to work on a close match, since bone marrow transplants have a very high risk factor.

When bone marrow is transplanted, the chances of survival—if the marrow donor is a sibling—stands at about 50-50. With an unrelated donor, the odds sink to 40-60. And the transplant *must* work the first time since lethal doses of chemotherapy and radiation are used to kill the diseased bone marrow before new marrow is injected. If a transplant patient survives a couple of years, the procedure could be repeated, but it cannot be done again right away, Susan said. The transplanted bone marrow must match in six antigen categories or rejection is almost certain. But even when the matches are made, the odds are still scary.

Since none of Susan's siblings matched, she had to look elsewhere for bone marrow. That's when she learned that only 600,000 of this country's 250 million people are registered. Since only healthy people between the ages of eighteen and fifty-five are accepted for screening, that eliminates a lot of people who might be willing.

When Susan's doctors checked the bank, however, they found fifty-two possible donors, but only because Susan is "a very common match." But what about those with rare types of bone marrow, where the odds can run as high as a million to one in finding one match? What about the black leukemia victims (where black donors are almost always more compatible) whose race makes up just 3 percent of the donors nationally?

To their credit, Susan and Jack (and their friends) set out to do something. They organized a "donor typing day" in Fort Valley, and 107 new names were added to the national bone marrow bank. Since typings—which are done through simple blood tests—cost about $65 per person, the Lees looked for a way to defray those expenses for potential donors. So they sold barbecue, some 800 plates at five dollars each. They paid all of the bills, and Susan Lee notched a victory that day.

Pauline Cantey
A Mother's Unwavering Love
(from a column published on Mother's Day, May 8, 1994)

BYRON—Melvin Cantey lived almost half a century. We'll never know for certain whether he thought those were good years or bad years. Born with severe birth defects, Melvin could never express his feelings in words. But if his actions—and, indeed, his affection for other human beings—were an indicator, then he lived forty-nine very good years.

People closest to him will tell you that he lived that long simply because of a mother's unwavering love. On this Mother's Day, there can be no better time to tell the story of Melvin and his mother, Pauline Cantey.

Pauline Williams of Macon and Richard Cantey of Hemingway, South Carolina, were married fifty-two years ago, and in the next five years, they had three children. Richard Jr., now of Crawford County, was the first-born, and Patsy Cantey Garrett of Stone Mountain was the baby. Melvin was born in between. The Cantey kids grew up in Macon's old Peach Orchard section, and while Richard and Patsy pursued an education in regular schools, Melvin became his mother's constant companion. At first, Melvin struggled through high fever and convulsions just to live. Many times, Pauline Cantey stayed up all night, holding her sick child—and praying.

When Melvin didn't walk at an early age, his mother bought one of those little merry-go-rounds and put him to walking beside it. He didn't walk until he was seven, but he *did* walk. It was a victory for a determined mother. Once he'd learned to walk, his mother put him in a school for handicapped children. "But they *made* my mother take him out of that school because he couldn't learn fast enough to suit them," Patsy told me. "It broke Mama's heart to have to do that."

She reflected a moment and then said, "If Melvin had been born forty years later, his life would have been different. He would have accomplished a lot more and maybe had a better life outside the home. But people were cruel to handicapped children back then. I can remember taking Melvin with me sometimes and other kids would make fun of him because he just made noises instead of talking."

Indeed, Melvin's vocabulary never got past the "mama and da-da" stage. However, Melvin sometimes amazed family members with his memory. "He loved baseball cards," Patsy said, "and if one was missing, he knew it and he would find a way to let us know." At his physical best, Melvin could play kick-ball in the yard with other kids.

Melvin also loved Christmas. He would sit for hours beside the family's Christmas tree, laughing happily as he gazed at the lights and presents. About ten years ago, doctors gave Melvin less than six months to live. The family put up an artificial tree that springtime so Melvin would have one last Christmas.

But Pauline Cantey worked that wonderful mother's magic again. Melvin pulled through. Melvin survived one crisis after another, always with his mother at his side. Even when she started having to use a walker to get around about five years ago, she still took care of her son. Medical folks were always quick to praise the care he'd been given at home, Patsy said. "She took care of him like he was a baby."

Eight weeks ago, Melvin was admitted to the Medical Center of Central Georgia. Five weeks ago, he was moved into the intensive care unit. I don't have to tell you where Pauline spent the past two months. She seldom went home and was at her son's bedside every possible minute.

Melvin's heart finally quit beating Thursday afternoon, and a very special relationship between mother and son came to an end after forty-nine years. He was buried Saturday, the day before Mother's Day.

Alice Smith
"Don't Mess with Mama"
(from a column published on February 19, 1993)

Get this picture in your mind: A man walks into a dining hall where the down-and-out-gather for a free meal. He pulls out a pistol. The man is confronted by a grandmotherly woman who stands little more than five feet tall. But her message is clear and concise: "We don't allow any of that (guns) in here," says the little woman. " Now take that thing and get out. You ain't getting anything to eat here, mister."

Sound like something straight out of the movies? Well, it isn't. It happened right here in our town at the Macon Outreach on Mulberry. That's just one of the stories which is told and re-told about Alice Smith, a lady whom just about everyone calls Mama.

"She really is the mother of this unit," says Nancylee Cater, executive director of the Outreach program. "She can handle any situation, and she does it with a smile. She's really quite amazing." Mama's journey to the Outreach dining hall is pretty amazing, too.

Alice Robinson Smith was born in Macon. She graduated at old Hudson High, and, after bringing a couple of children into the world, she started working at the Medical Center of Central Georgia in 1959 as a nurse's aide. In twenty-six years, she moved up to other jobs. She became a clerk in the emergency room, and that piqued her interest to become an emergency medical technician. She rode ambulances into her fiftieth year on earth.

In early 1985, a heart bypass operation ended her EMT career, and other medical problems forced her retirement. In five years, Alice underwent ten operations, most of which would be called "major" surgery. "I've had so many surgeries that, when the Lord meets me, he's going to ask, 'Where are all of the moving parts?' "

While she fought back physically, she also looked after her eighty-year-old husband, Grady, who is a diabetic and must also have regular kidney dialysis treatments.

But Alice, who works as hard at home and for Congregational Baptist Church as she does at her job, was not used to inactivity. She says she just *had* to find something more to do with herself. So she volunteered to work at the Middle Georgia Community Food Bank. She also worked in the VISTA program and Project READ, an adult literacy program.

In July 1990, she was asked to fill in for a couple of weeks while the regular cook at Macon Outreach took a vacation. She never left. In fact, she soon took over the operation.

When Mrs. Cater was named executive director at Macon Outreach, she was pleased with what she found. "Alice takes care of everything in there (the dining hall)," she said. "She does the paperwork, all of the purchasing, all of the running around. . . . Her car gets more miles on it than the church van. In fact, there isn't much this lady hasn't done, and there isn't much this lady can't do."

Indeed, Alice must be as much diplomat as cook. "All of those workers out there (in the kitchen and dining hall) except Alice are volunteers," Mrs. Cater said. "You have to know how to get along with people to keep them working like Alice does." Most of the volunteers who help in the kitchen and clean up the dining hall come from the ranks of approximately 125 people who show up each day looking for a hot meal. And Alice is obviously liked and respected by everyone—except maybe those who would tote guns and knives into her little world.

"I understand these people," she said. "They are frustrated with life. They have to be frustrated to live under a bridge or on the street. But they're still our brothers, and we have to take care of them."

Even those who break the rules are generally treated "lovingly," Alice said. "And they can't stand that," she said with a smile. "They've been abused so much that they don't know how to deal with kindness . . . except to be nice, too."

When she deals with others, the smile is almost always there. But the message has been passed along: Don't mess with Mama. Nancylee Cater regarded her kitchen supervisor with a serious expression and said, "That lady has an attitude. . ." Then her face broke into a big smile and she added, "The right one!"

8

STORIES OF TRUE GRIT:
THEY SUCCEEDED
AGAINST ALL ODDS

In twenty-five years, I have written some pretty remarkable success stories about people who persevered and reached their goals in spite of blindness, crippling diseases, in spite of any setback—indeed, they succeeded in spite of it all.

Gayle Ogilvie
A Woman of Quiet Courage
(from a column first published in 1979)

HAZLEHURST—Since most of us never need more than a couple of aspirin to kill a hangover, it's difficult for us to understand how anyone can put up with excruciating pain day after day. Gayle Ogilvie didn't know what life without pain could be like until recently.

Folks in Hazlehurst told me about Gayle. They called her gallant, courageous, and determined. Mentally, she could whip a tiger, they said. Physically, she could hardly walk. I can't imagine what her life has been like. That's why I went to Hazlehurst and talked to Gayle and her parents, Charlie and Ouida Ogilvie.

Almost twenty-one years ago, doctors first diagnosed rheumatic fever and rheumatoid arthritis—diseases of the elderly not usually found in a five-year-old girl. The first thing doctors did was send her to bed for nine months. Gayle did what the doctors said, and that's one reason she started school on time in the fall of 1959. You have to admire this young lady. She never failed a grade and never missed a day of school unnecessarily.

At times, she had to be lifted into the school bus because her arthritic joints would not let her climb even a couple of steps. But she hung onto life with a steely grip that amazed those around her. She made numerous trips to the hospital, including one to kick the cortisone habit. But the drug that had dulled the pain also stunted her growth to the point that she was just 4 feet, 7 inches tall and weighed a mere seventy-five pounds at age twenty-six.

Her size brought embarrassing questions. Ouida Ogilvie remembers, "Gayle has a beautiful voice and often sang with a quartet. But people kept asking, 'How old is that little girl?' even when she was older than some of those asking questions."

Gayle gave up public singing, and the ever-spreading arthritis eventually robbed her of the nimble fingers she once used to play the piano. Still, she has more going for her than those who talked about her size.

Life always has been a constant battle. She developed an ulcer when her friends were getting braces. She fell and broke her back when girls her age were leading cheers at the local high school. In spite of it all, Gayle went to secretarial school, graduated and got a good job with the transportation section at Hazlehurst Mills. A doctor once praised Gayle's courage this way: "If I had been her, I would have jumped off a bridge a long time ago."

By 1978, the huge doses of medication had caused Gayle's height to shrink to just 4-feet-3. But she sought relief in the only way she could without going back to cortisone. At Scottish Rite Hospital in Atlanta, surgeons rebuilt her joints with plastic and steel.

After operations on a shoulder, two knees, two feet, and two elbows, she went home to fading pain and a desire to return to work. Doctor bills needed to be paid and she's used to making her own way. In fact, her determination to finish high school, graduate from business school, and get a job surely saved her family from financial ruin, her mother said: "If Gayle hadn't worked and helped pay the bills and if she hadn't had good insurance, we wouldn't have a roof over our heads," she said.

But Gayle did work, and her courage attracted a multitude of friends who often rallied to her cause. The Pilot Club lit a Christmas tree for her, and CBers hawked donations for her over the airwaves.

Gayle would still like to have her hands operated on, but she says medicine has not progressed far enough yet. But she's young enough she can still hope.

And we can hope with her.

Footnote: Gayle is married to Leon Barber and still lives in Hazlehurst. Both of her parents are deceased.

Paul Sprinkle
His Range of Skills Is Amazing
(from a column published on January 28, 1996)

Without these hearing aids, I can barely hear thunder. But I can plug a little modern technology into my ears and go about my business, and people hardly notice that I wear them. Paul Sprinkle of Macon isn't as fortunate. His eyes are plastic, and he sees nothing. Still, he goes about his business as though he can see as well as you and I.

His means of making a living, like that of many blind people, is tuning, repairing and rebuilding pianos. But even among blind people, Paul is a pretty amazing person. And cheerful? Paul is as upbeat as anyone I've ever met. He's hooked on life and going at it full throttle.

I can't imagine what it would be like to live in eternal darkness, but if you've never had sight. . . .

Paul Willis Sprinkle, age forty-one, was the only child born to the marriage of Jack and Eva Sprinkle. His father, a piano tuner, was blinded early in life by retinoblastoma, a cancer that destroys the retina of the eye. It is hereditary.

Paul can't remember ever seeing anything. He was blind in infancy. His parents divorced when Paul was six years old. His father went on to become well known in his field. He lived in Arlington, Georgia until his death a year ago, and at one time, he tuned pianos in the White House.

But Paul talks most affectionately of Everett Oddie, his stepfather and "the man who raised me." His stepfather, also a legally blind piano tuner, wasted no time in teaching Paul the business. "I remember him sitting me in the key bed of a grand piano, giving me some tools and telling me to start taking out the screws (that held together the inner workings of the piano)," Paul recalls.

Of course, he attended schools wherever the family lived—Washington, D.C., Chicago, and Batavia, New York. And he learned a lot of skills that let him live independently. He learned to take care of himself, walk alone four blocks to school with the use of a cane, type on a braille typewriter, and, yes, to tune pianos.

It amazes people that Paul can simply feel a piano or listen to the sound of the bass keys and tell the brand name. But that's just a small part of this man's skills.

He can completely dismantle any piano and know what has to be replaced among the hundreds of pieces of metal, wood and felt. And he can do the work.

His skills were honed while he lived in New York. "We'd buy up old pianos and those needing extensive repairs," he said, "and, then, during the harsh winters when we couldn't get out much, we'd repair and rebuild them. Each one of those pianos was a learning experience."

Paul learned to do quality work, and it bothers him when he finds that someone has cut corners by using synthetic materials to make repairs.

The stepfather who reared him passed away in 1978, and Paul moved to Macon with his mother after she remarried. For a while, he worked for others, but for the past fifteen years, he has operated his own business.

In the house he shares with his mother and stepfather in north Macon, half a dozen pianos are in various stages of repair. But there's more to Paul Sprinkle than what he can do to those pianos.

For instance, he can bowl. Using a special handrail for guidance, he has bowled as high as 164. He also has delved deeply into geography and birds. He has "traveled" around the world with thirty-year-old maps done in braille. He learned the calls of hundreds of birds on four continents by listening to cassettes he received as a long ago Christmas present.

Extensive projects don't intimidate Paul. It took five years for him to "read" the entire Talking World Book Encyclopedia, but he did it. "It was an adventure," he says. Grant Fossum, who sometimes drives Paul to a tuning job, says, "I never want for a subject to have a good conversation with him. His knowledge of the world is fantastic."

Needless to say, Paul is special to people who know him—his friends and customers. But they are special to him, too. After he finishes a tuning or repair job, he goes to a braille typewriter in his upstairs "headquarters" and makes extensive notes. When he goes back to tune a piano a second time, he reviews those notes on both the piano and the people so he can be on familiar ground.

Are there more goals to reach, more tasks to be conquered? "Yes!" Paul says enthusiastically. "I'd like to learn computers, but they are very expensive. And I'd like to travel."

That's what I admire most about Paul. He dreams of new horizons, even though he is now an insulin-dependent diabetic and even though everyone in his household is legally blind and he must depend on others to get him across town to tune a piano.

When a person sets his or her sights beyond the obvious capabilities. . . . Well, you know the rest of that line.

Djamel Tlemsani
No Dream Too Big for Him
(from a column published on February 17, 1992)

Djamel Tlemsani has the kind of life's dream that makes an old man want to remember and want to dream youthful dreams again, too.

Of course, I have no business doing that. I've pretty well reached my station in life. I'll never fly to the moon or become a famous actor, surgeon, or architect.

But Djamel might. In fact, I give him a better chance of being anything he wants to be—of indeed reaching some unreachable goal—than I would the everyday grammar-school genius out there. And I'm saying that even though Djamel is deaf. You would have to communicate directly with this brilliant twelve-year-old to understand why I say that. Until you can do that, you'll just have to listen to Ol' Boyd talk about him.

Djamel is the eldest of three sons of Hamza Tlemsani, an Algerian-born engineer now working with a Macon firm, and Sonya Galloway Tlemsani, a native of Albertville, Alabama. Like his younger brother, Mourad, Djamel was born with an acute hearing loss. He can be classified as stone deaf. Although he wears a couple of powerful hearing aids, he says he hears only very powerful noises.

He was born in Atlanta, but he has lived all but the first year of his life in Macon. Like most deaf children, he started school at age two so he could learn sign language before trying to mainstream in public schools.

In Djamel's case, mainstreaming was an adventure, not a handicap. In spite of his hearing loss, his teachers offer only the highest praise for his ability to learn. Kitty LaFountain says,

"Djamel is in elementary school, but he challenges us (the teachers). He's just a very smart young fellow."

He's indeed smart enough that Mrs. LaFountain isn't making any more bets concerning geography. She lost a twenty-five-cent wager to Djamel about which was the largest city, Atlanta or Miami. (If you don't know, I'll let you look up that one.)

But Djamel is a whiz on more than just geography. Consider that his math skills border on genius. He can spell just about any word in the dictionary. In fact, in 1991, when he was in Brookdale School, he won the spelling bee in spite of having to "hear" the words from a teacher using sign-words.

He came close again this year at Rosa Taylor School, and Mrs. LaFountain considers the preparation for that test as one of her own great experiences. "There were 1,000 very difficult words," she said, "and there were no signs for most of them. Djamel and I invented our own signs for the first 150, but since we only had four hours to prepare, we didn't get through the entire list." Djamel missed on "porridge" when he mistook it for "parish." He knew how to spell that word, his teacher said. There just wasn't a sign for "porridge."

With his life uncluttered by MTV or the endless list of mindless television shows, Djamel spends a lot of time at the family's home computer and reading all sorts of books filled with facts, statistics, and other data.

Of course—in case you haven't guessed by now—Djamel makes straight A's. Well, he did make one B last year, but Djamel says that won't happen again. He has a special incentive this year. His dad has promised a $100 reward for a perfect report card. Djamel says he is determined to do it. He already has plans for $75 of that windfall—to buy a huge map to take him on imaginary trips around the world.

What does this deaf genius want to be? An astronaut. He wants to be the first man to walk on Mars. Did I say something about lofty dreams? Just don't count Djamel Tlemsani out of anything.

Bud and Elise Rhodes
Blind Couple's Vision Comes True
(from a column on June 30, 1985)

PINEVIEW—The modern, brown and yellow ranch-type house on the outskirts of Pineview was built with "blind sight." It isn't perfect, but it's certainly comfortable. Some minor finishing touches may be needed, but it's still one of the best-looking houses around Pineview. And the frame home is appreciated by its occupants because it was built the early American way—stick by stick as its builders could afford materials.

But the most remarkable thing about this 2,176-square-foot-house is that it was built by Bud Rhodes, a completely blind man, and his wife, Elise, who is also blind in the "legal" sense. I first wrote about Bud and Elise in the fall of 1976, when only the shell of the house was up. But they promised they'd live in it one day. And now they do.

True romance has lasted more than thirty-five years for Bud and Elise. Even now, they hold hands for reasons other than blindness. They met at the Georgia Academy for the Blind in Macon. He finished school there in the spring of 1949. When he left, he married Elise and took her home to peaceful Pineview, a farming community nestled between Hawkinsville and Pitts in northern Wilcox County. They took up residence in an old farmhouse a mile outside Pineview and reared three children. Bud made a living with a combination of enterprises—from hog farming to tuning pianos.

It always has been important to Bud and Elise that they make their own way and keep the bills paid. But along with that resolve, they have kept a sense of humor. For instance, Bud, who lost his eyes as well as his eyesight in a childhood accident at age eight, once shook up some folks in Pineview by driving a farm truck through town. Well, he wasn't actually driving it. A long-armed friend barely peeked over the dashboard and guided the truck from the lower part of the steering wheel. People still laugh about how the streets quickly cleared when the word spread that blind Bud was driving a truck down main street.

Bud often amazes people with his awareness. For instance, I once asked him to tell me which direction he was facing. He quickly—and accurately—said, "North."

Oh, there were times he needed a little help. For instance, he would ask his children to describe each of the sows in his pens.

Since he could easily distinguish the noises of one from the other with his keen sense of hearing, he once shocked a visitor when he called a particular hog by its name and told it to stop all of that grunting. "You actually know which hog made that sound?" the surprised visitor asked. "Certainly," answered Bud, "the gray one with the black spots." That visitor helped a legend grow by telling the story around Wilcox and Pulaski counties.

Few local people doubted Bud when he said that he and Elise were going to build their own house. They fully expected that it would have square corners, level floors, and perfectly placed paneling. Anyone who knew the gutsy resolve of this couple knew Bud and Elise would succeed.

Bud used skills he picked up as a child to drive nails and measure boards. His parents treated him "just like any other child." Since he preferred a hammer and nails to regular toys, driving nails was no big deal to this blind man when it came to building a house.

He's quite amazing in other aspects of building, too. For instance, I once picked up a board, handed it to Bud and asked, "How long is it?"

"Mighty close to forty inches," he answered.

Was it just a ballpark guess? I don't think so. The board measured 39-7/8 inches. Elise, who'd never used a circular saw until the house-building project began, soon became adept at cutting even the most difficult angles, despite having very limited eyesight.

Nothing seemed to deter the Rhodeses. To them, building their own home was a great adventure, and they took the time to enjoy it. They built as they could afford the materials. When money ran low, they stopped for a while.

They hired people only to lay the foundation and roof the house. Bud explained those decisions simply. "There's nothing more important than a good foundation, and I didn't think we knew enough about it. As for the roof, I didn't think a blind man had any business up there."

So last week we sat in the yellow and brown house and talked about things important to a blind couple who can build a house. Elise, who is also nearly deaf, busied herself making a pot of coffee. Unable to keep the fondness out of his voice, Bud said, "Thirty-five years. That's too long to put up with one woman." Then he smiled and added, "Of course, if her hearing was good, I might not say that quite so bravely."

About building his own home, he held out his hands and said, "There's a lot of built-in senses in these. You know, I wish I had the money to build another house so I could capitalize off my mistakes." He gestured at things he's never seen and added, "We're still working on the house. As long as it isn't finished, we have something in front of us, something to think about."

Their five grandchildren are often mentioned, too. "This house is way too big for the two of us, but when the grandkids get here, we need 6,000 square feet."

About toiling for five years before they ever lived in the house, Bud said, "I never doubted that we'd finish it. We *had* to.

At times, it looked pretty bleak, but we just kept at it. You know, each job was a lot more fun *after* we'd finished it."

With that he smiled, reached for Elise's hand and squeezed it, a sure sign of affection for the "eyes" of this house-building couple.

Butch Redmond
Ambassador to a Small Town
(from a column published on October 18, 1993)

For fifty years, the Redmond family knocked on any door with a tragedy behind it. Goodhearted and responsive, they called on the hurt, the dying, the bereaved. They brought cakes, comfort and kind words. Now, the people of Cochran find themselves walking to a door with tragedy behind it—the brick Redmond home on Second Street a few blocks south of the business district.

Wylene, Butch's mother and guardian and teacher, the light of his life. . . . Wylene Stokes Redmond died Tuesday afternoon of an heart attack. She was buried Friday. A family—and indeed a town—huddled around Butch.

Butch. When you say that name in Cochran, you don't have to put a last name with it, and folks will smile. They smile because Butch, who was born without the mental capacity you and I have, is the town's ambassador. He sprinkles cheer along streets like so much confetti.

Now with both of his parents dead, one question is being asked all over Cochran: What happens to Butch? Family members are seeking a solution—hopefully, a solution that will keep Butch in Cochran. I'll tell you about that, but first, listen to Butch's story from the beginning.

He was born Charles Curry Redmond Jr. on March 22, 1956. He was the only child of Charles and Wylene Redmond. Although Butch would never learn to read and write, he went to public schools for twelve years and learned something perhaps more valuable to him than written words and numbers. He learned to get along with people.

Because he liked people, he fit right in with his parents' goodhearted ways. Anyone in Cochran will tell you that, when tragedy struck, the Redmonds were usually the first to ring the doorbell, leave some food and ask what else they could do.

When Charles Redmond died in 1976, every man in town became Butch's daddy—at least, a little bit. Butch got into the habit of making daily rounds through downtown Cochran, chatting with people and saying things like, "You look just like your sister" or "Where did you get that new car?"

That's one of the things about Butch. Although his mind is less than adequate, he is blessed with a remarkable memory. He never forgets a name, and he knows what kind of car just about everyone in town drives.

Less than a year ago, Wylene said this about her son: "Butch doesn't have any hobbies . . . except talking to people. He doesn't read. He will always be a baby. But he's very compassionate, and he's truly concerned about others." She also told me that she worried sometimes about what would happen to Butch after she was gone. But she told me that she believed that "everything is taken care of." She told others the same thing. Although she never spelled out her plan, she told family, friends and neighbors that Butch would have good care.

This week, Jim Redmond of Atlanta, Butch's cousin, said he and other relatives have been sifting through files and talking to an attorney "to try to put things together for Butch." He also sought to dispel a rumor in Cochran that Butch was going to be put in a group home for the mentally retarded in Macon.

"We're going to try very hard to find a solution that would keep Butch in this house, preferably with some member of the family living here," he said. "If not, then we will try to find someone outside the family to live with him."

Former mayor Charles Killebrew attended Wylene's funeral and said what most of Cochran has been thinking, "I hope it works out. Cochran would really miss Butch if he had to move."

Willie Basby, a city council member and Army reservist who also attended the funeral, got a good lesson in Redmond kindness during the Persian Gulf War.

"I spent a year over there," he said, "and they were always sending cards, flowers or candy to me. They were that kind of people. I hope things work out for Butch."

So do I. So does an entire town.

Mike Hobbs
He Can; He Does
(from a column published on September 23, 1990)

For Mike Hobbs, there is no place in his life for that oft-used phrase "I can't." Never has been; never will be. His mother told him early in life not to use that phrase. So he didn't. He didn't use it when he went to school. He didn't use it when he went deer hunting. He didn't use it when he went job hunting. He's never used it despite being born thirty-five years ago without hands or feet, with only stubs where arms and legs should have been. So let me tell you a story about pride, honor, determination, and success.

Mike was the last of four boys born to Roger and Hazel Hobbs. He was a twin and his brother, Richard, "is normal—if you want to use that phrase," Mike says. But then he asks, "What is normal anyhow?"

Certainly, his mother didn't bother to make a distinction. "She made me feel like I was just one of the boys, never showed me any partiality," he recalled.

He was fitted with artificial limbs and sent to school, and he was expected to make good grades. He did all right. "Of course, I was always having to prove myself to others—students and teachers—but once they got to know me, we got along fine."

Looking back at his childhood, he said, "Handicapped means not being able to do things. Well, the only thing that I wanted to do that I didn't was learn to ride a bicycle."

After graduating at Southwest High in 1973, he went to Macon College to study accounting. He didn't find a job right away, he said, "because, in the real world, some people have a hard time accepting handicapped people." So he took a job where the people he dealt with wouldn't know his condition. He conducted telephone surveys for a radio station. He also did some gunsmithing.

And he took up deer hunting. He has hunted with both rifle and crossbow and he has made numerous kills, including a nine-pointer in 1977. It's really something to hear him tell stories about how he carries his rifle, how he holds it like a right-hander but pulls the trigger with his left stub, how he cocks a cross-bow, and how he shimmies up a tree into a deer stand.

When Rodney Selman, a student at Mercer University, heard about Mike a couple of years ago, he turned engineering class projects into inventions for Mike. He designed a special harness to carry Mike's rifle and other contraptions that make Mike's hunting trips less dependent on others.

About ten years ago, Mike applied for a job at Robins Air Force Base. On July 6, 1981, he was hired as an accounting technician.

If you're wondering how well Mike Hobbs earns his way, all you have to do is talk to those who know him. They use words like "amazing," "remarkable," and "capable" to describe him.

He didn't come looking for a handout at the base and he didn't get one. He pulls his own weight, answering three-fourths of the calls that come in at the Travel and Finance Office and operating computers just like anyone else.

How does he manage all this?

Well, he may have to get around in a wheelchair, but you ought to see this guy pick up a pen between his two arm stubs and write as legibly as most school teachers.

So where is Mike's life going? For one thing, he has found "a very special" female companion. And it will give you the warm fuzzies just to see Mike blush when he talks about her. For another, he's having a car outfitted with special controls so he can drive. It's something he's always wanted to do, something to which he never said "can't".

Finally, there is the CPR class. Yep, Mike took and *passed* that wonderful lifesaving course just a couple of weeks ago.

Yeah, yeah, I know. I ought to shut up and stop bragging on this guy for a while, but I just can't.

Oh, Lord, did I say "can't"? Forgive me, Mike Hobbs.

Debbie Andrews Youghn
Extraordinary Survivor
(from a column published July 10, 1994)

FORSYTH—The first time I heard Debbie Andrews's voice, it came from inside a sterile bubble in a Houston, Tex., hospital where she was fighting leukemia. On a telephone, the voice sounded very young and very scared. "I want to come home," she said. Weeks later, Debbie, then fifteen, came home. She was thin and washed out from extensive chemotherapy and being confined to a sterile bubble for ninety days. Still, she managed a smile and said, "I'm going to be okay."

Ten months later, she proved that she was indeed OK by running a foot-race with a neighborhood boy. Six months after the foot-race, she told me that she was on a diet. She'd gained back so much weight that she was afraid the boys at Mary Persons High wouldn't notice her.

And four years after I first called the girl in the sterile bubble, Debbie, then nineteen, was in the hospital again. But this time, she was in a Macon hospital to give birth to twin daughters, Tracey and Leighanne.

Doctors who specialized in leukemia treatment said at the time that Debbie was one of a very few leukemia patients ever to give birth at all, since chemo tends to render patients sterile. Debbie was the first ever to bear twins, they said.

But that was a long time ago. In less than a month, the twins will turn fifteen, Debbie's age when leukemia struck. But Debbie told me during a visit last week that she harbors no real fear for her daughters' health since leukemia is not a hereditary malady. Then she added, "When I look at them and realize that's the age I was when it happened . . oh, yes, it scares me a little."

But any frown left from a conversation about that gives way to a warm smile when she talks about the way thousands of people rallied around her when they heard about her illness in the summer of 1975. "People really were nice," she said. Indeed, they were. They donated more than $12,000 to help her workaday parents cope with bills and the expense of staying in Houston where they were *needed*.

You see, when Debbie was at her weakest, medical folks hooked up one of her family members to a machine that simply transferred blood from their bodies to hers. It was a last-ditch effort to save her life, and the blood transferred to her family members could be rebuilt in a matter of hours by healthy systems.

Folks back home also sent so many get-well cards that she could cover the walls of her hospital room several times over. When she came home, the Andrews's house in Forsyth was overrun with well-wishers, while hundreds more just drove slowly past to let the girl inside know that they cared.

She went into remission and stayed there, but it was the birth of the twins on August 5, 1979, that catapulted her into the national spotlight. Her story was carried across the country by wire services. Pictures of Debbie and her two healthy babies appeared in hundreds of newspapers.

When the hullaballoo finally died down, Debbie led a more private life. She worked at the Monroe County Hospital for thirteen years, starting as a clerk and working her way up to a job as a physical therapist.

She also suffered some of the more common setbacks in life. She and the twins' father were divorced about a year after the girls were born, and for nine years, she lived the life of a single parent. The twins grew up quietly in Forsyth where folks didn't make any big deal over this rare set of twins.

In 1989, Debbie married Tony Youghn, a lab technician at the Bibb Company, and, less than a year later, he adopted the twins, then nine years old. Debbie told me the other day that the disease has been giving her the dreads lately. "For a long time, I didn't worry about it," she said,"but now . . . we have such a perfect family. . . . We're so happy . . . I don't want anything to spoil that."

The only thing that bothers her, she said, is that people have sometimes asked her why she is so lucky that she has been in remission for nineteen years and is blessed with twin daughters while so many other leukemia patients do not survive. "I don't know what to say when they ask that," she said, "but I do believe the Lord likes me and has a reason for me being here."

As the twins near fifteen, they look like anything but twins. Leighanne is several inches taller than Tracey. Tracey has very dark hair while Leighanne's is a light brown. Leighanne wears eyeglasses; Tracey doesn't. But they are alike in some ways. Both are good students, their mother said, and both are crackerjack softball players.

Debbie says her daughters are about as normal as teenage girls can be. "They're typical," Debbie said."They're boy-crazy, and they like to talk on the phone."

After what she's been through, Debbie Andrews Youghn will take all of the "normal" and "typical" she can get.

9

THE MENNONITES:
FAITH, FAMILY, AND FARMING

*T*he Mennonites of Macon County form an island of abiding faith and simplicity in the midst of social upheaval and moral decay. Desperately, they hold on to a way of life that is not influenced by television, politics, the Internet, or drugs. For twenty-five years, I have admired their determination to hold off the onslaught of permissiveness as they raise their young to carry on a way of life that is so different from yours and mine. They became a permanent part of my life when Wanda, my wonderful daughter, joined their church—and their way of life—in 1996. I hope this series of articles, published in 1997, will help spread understanding about this devoutly religious group of people.

A History of the Mennonite Movement

Who are the Mennonites? The Mennonite church was established during the Reformation, a period in the sixteenth century that marked the rise of Protestantism in western Europe.

This religious tradition bears the name of Menno Simons (1496-1561), a Dutchman who was a Catholic priest for eleven years before turning to the Anabaptist movement in 1535. He was baptized by Obbe Philips, founder of Dutch Anabaptists, and named a bishop in that faith. For seven years, he traveled the Netherlands, preaching "the simplicity and purity of the apostolic church."

In a part of the world that was solidly Roman Catholic, Simons became such a powerful voice that in 1542 Emperor Charles V placed a bounty on his head. But Simons's efforts were not to be deterred. He moved from country to country in western Europe, and he published seven books to help him spread the gospel.

His followers, described in history books as "nonresistant" and "nonviolent," first became known as "Mennists" and as their ranks grew, so did persecution. Between 1531 and 1597, some 2,000 martyrs were put to death in the Netherlands alone, and three quarters of those were Mennonites. The early Mennonites were called Anabaptists (rebaptizers) because they refused to recognize infant baptism and insisted on "believer's baptism" only.

Simons died on a sickbed on January 31, 1561, but he left behind a religious legacy that was destined to survive in spite of harsh and sometimes deadly persecution. By 1700, the Dutch

Mennonites could count 160,000 people who had been baptized into their faith. A hundred years later, there were fewer than 27,000 after Dutch Mennonites fled in droves, mostly to Russia and the United States.

A couple of centuries later, the Russian government revoked a military exemption for Mennonites, spurring a huge exodus from Russia. Those who were left behind were shot, exiled, or forced to recant their faith.

Soon after the turn of this century, the Mennonite Church no longer existed in Russia. Most had immigrated to Canada and the United States. The first thirteen families that landed in this country came at the behest of William Penn, who invited Mennonite immigrants to settle in Pennsylvania, where the king of England had granted him an extensive tract of land.

Those first thirteen families arrived in October 1683 and established a community called Germantown, not far from Philadelphia. They are described in history books as "peaceful people who persecuted no one, took no part in any war and never followed the folly and fashion of the world."

However, that small enclave of Mennonites didn't mind setting a precedent when they felt that the cause was just. Five years after their arrival, the Mennonites mounted the first protest in this country against slavery. Such a move did not sit well with some of the more wealthy residents of the region, especially since the richest people often owned the most slaves, and the Mennonites paid a price. They got little help from outsiders.

Their deprivation was such that Germantown was nick-named "Armentown" or Poortown. They struggled to erect houses, clear land, grow crops, and provide for their children. However, the Mennonites persevered, the history books say, and by the early 1700s, they were at the center of a flourishing economy around Germantown.

In 1709, a steady stream of immigrants from Switzerland began settling in a nearby area that is now known as Lancaster County. More than 500 families eventually came. The descendants of those families still live there and are known as the Old Order Amish. Even in the 1990s, they travel in horse-drawn buggies and shun such conveniences as electricity.

Immigration slowed in the latter part of the 1700s, and some Mennonites chose to resettle in western Pennsylvania and Ohio while others moved southward to Maryland and Virginia.

One of those groups was the Beachy Mennonites, a group that broke away from the Old Order Amish and followed the teachings of Bishop Mose Beachy. They were a progressive group that lived near Norfolk, Virginia, and favored mechanized farming, considered a radical departure from the old way of life. Even though the Beachy Mennonites were sometimes criticized by the Old Order Amish as "too liberal," change came slowly for those people, too, the history books say.

After World War II, the Virginia Mennonites watched from their farm fields as airplanes buzzed overhead, busy highways bisected their farms and non-Mennonite settlements crept ever closer. As Mennonite farm families grew in size, more land was needed for children growing into adulthood, so they began looking elsewhere.

And that is why in 1953, three carloads of Mennonite men came to Georgia to try to find a new paradise where land was plentiful and the countryside was quiet. They chose to settle in Macon County, and about 140 Mennonite families now live there. Those 550 souls worship in three churches, and they still follow the religious doctrine that Menno Simons preached more than 450 years ago.

Yesterday and Today

Donny Swartzentruber, a tall and bearded thirty-seven-year-old Mennonite farmer and minister wearing garb that was appropriate a century ago, stood in his back yard on a hot summer afternoon and watched as an airplane swooped low overhead. He waved, knowing that the pilot of the crop-duster would see him and know who was waving. After all, it was Swartzentruber's cotton field that was being dusted.

A couple of miles away, eighty-six-year-old Sol Yoder Sr. talked about why he and other Mennonites moved to Macon County from Virginia forty-four years earlier. "Too many airplanes," he said. "There was noise all the time." What was once a nuisance in Virginia is now merely a curiosity for a new generation of Macon County Mennonites.

This new generation, most of whom were born here, are a blend of the old and the new. They hold on to many of the old Mennonite ways from dress code to the way children are educated, and they shun many things that are an everyday part of life in the outside world. There are no television sets, no beauty salons, no alcoholic beverages. As a rule, change is tolerated only in very small doses. Still, change is marching at a scary and relentless pace into their lives, and that distresses most Mennonites.

Yoder still clearly recalls how life changed in the countryside just outside Norfolk, Virginia, where a large community of Beachy Mennonites lived in peace for decades. "After the war (World War II) ended," he said, "that area began growing in leaps and bounds. They really came at us, buying up farms, building houses. Jet planes were roaring overhead. We couldn't stand in our yards and talk."

Yoder, still active and alert as he approaches his eighty-seventh birthday, recalls how three carloads of Mennonite men came to Georgia on a land-hunting expedition in 1953. Their first stop was Americus, he said, and then they visited Smithville, Lilly and Vienna. The Mennonites were at the courthouse in Vienna checking soil samples when a man said he had a farm for sale near Montezuma. "That's the first time I remember hearing Montezuma mentioned," Yoder said.

As it turned out, the man who said he had a farm for sale changed his mind, but the Mennonites were not discouraged. They chose to put up at a hotel in Montezuma and look around. As word spread about the purpose of their visit, Yoder remembers that "old people whose children didn't come back to farm started talking to us."

That visit marked the first time many Macon countians had ever seen a Mennonite, Yoder said. "One man saw us coming through the door (of a local dairy) and said, 'Here comes Jesus.' He took off running toward the back door and ran right into another (Mennonite)."

Most folks around Montezuma warmed to the newcomers right away, Yoder said, and by the time the group returned to Virginia, four Mennonites besides himself had taken options on farms east of Montezuma. Malon Weaver, Rudy Yoder (Sol's brother), Crist Yoder Sr. and Jonas Hershberger were the other buyers.

As Mennonites streamed into Macon County, they brought a strong faith in God with them. The Montezuma Mennonite Church congregation was founded in 1953 and held its first services in an abandoned community house built in the 1930s as part of the Flint River Farms Project. Thirty-eight members brought their own chairs and attended the first service on October 11, 1953.

In Macon County, those first Mennonites quickly established themselves as proficient farmers. They worked hard and paid their bills on time, and that endeared them to bankers and merchants alike. While they dressed like Old Order Amish, most were progressive in their farming methods. Sol Yoder recalled that he brought the first mechanized cotton picker to Macon County.

But those early Mennonite farmers didn't want to be viewed as too progressive, Swartzentruber recalled. "One of our men was at the John Deere dealership, looking at a six-row cultivator. Someone there said, 'A six-row cultivator? Those Mennonites are really getting up in the world, aren't they?' "

"When we heard about that," Swartzentruber said, "we cut all of our four-row cultivators in half and farmed with two-row cultivators."

Changes in church doctrine have never come quick and easy for Mennonites, and some of the changes are especially hard for the older generation to accept. "Our grandparents would flip over (in their graves) if they could see some of the things that are going on," said Lloyd Swartzentruber, age sixty-five, who moved his family to Macon County in 1957. "If outsiders don't have a high regard for us, it's because we're not practicing our religion."

It is, said Bishop Noah Yoder of Clearview Mennonite Church, a "constant struggle" to keep out influences that might dilute the purity and simplicity of the Mennonite way of life.

One change has especially chipped away at the very foundation of the Mennonite lifestyle. Too many Mennonite men no longer work on the farms. In fact, both of Sol Yoder's sons work elsewhere, and the rolling 472-acre tract of land he once cultivated now belongs to someone else, someone who is not even a Mennonite.

Jobs away from the farm can be very good or very bad, community leaders say, depending on how the increasing number of Mennonite men who work in the trades and factory jobs conduct themselves.

On the one hand, jobs in the secular community have driven twin spikes into the heart of the Mennonite way of life. First, fathers who are no longer close at hand do not exert the same influence on the young as those who work alongside their children on farms. Second, temptations away from the farm can be disastrous to marriages, church leaders say. A few Mennonite men have left their families and the church after taking jobs outside the community, and church leaders see this as a threat to a religious doctrine that does not tolerate infidelity or divorce.

On the other hand, Mennonite men who work in the trades—carpenters, welders, house builders—are highly regarded for their skills and work ethic, said Peter Whitt, principal at Montezuma Mennonite School. Besides making a respectable wage in the outside world, Whitt said those who follow their Mennonite upbringing will witness for the Lord among non-Mennonites.

About twenty of sixty Mennonite "heads of households" now work away from the farm, community leaders estimate. Since even more of the next generation are expected to seek jobs away from the farm, Mennonite schools already are gearing up to cope with the future, educators say. Some Mennonites say any change is bad, and they point to recent changes in church rules as a reason for moral decay.

For many years, Macon County Mennonites could not own cameras or possess pictures of themselves. They cited Scripture about "graven images" as the reason. However, that changed about eight years ago on a vote by the church congregation (which must approve all changes). For more than thirty years, Macon County Mennonites drove nothing but black cars and trucks. They believed flashy cars only fueled egos, and that went against the grain of the humble Mennonite image they desired.

Now, Mennonites own cars of several colors, but, still, they must be bland colors like white, black, dark blue or dark brown and four-door cars are preferred in order to eliminate sports cars and others that might be deemed too showy.

Although two-way walkie-talkies have been approved for use, radios that receive commercial stations in car or home are strictly forbidden. So while millions of Americans pay dearly to have the latest stereos installed in their automobiles, Mennonites pay to have factory-installed radios removed.

The dress code has undergone some rather subtle changes, too, and it varies from church to church. While men may now wear shirts with collars, most still favor the wearing of suspenders rather than belts. Colors must be subdued. Most designer clothing is not acceptable. Women still wear high-neckline dresses with hems that fall to the middle of the calf, and their hair—which is never cut—is put up beneath little white caps.

Computers are finding their way into the tight-knit community, too. Levi Mast, bishop at Gospel Light Mennonite Church, said the use of computers is being "carefully monitored." Also, they may not be connected to the Internet, he said, nor are computer games allowed. While Macon County's Mennonites live in modern homes and enjoy most of the everyday conveniences, television sets are still strictly forbidden. Mennonite leaders agree that the ban will not be lifted anytime soon.

How serious is the ban? Any Mennonite who might insist on owning a television set would "forfeit their church membership," said Noah Yoder, bishop at Clearview Mennonite Church.

Even though many taken-for-granted secular conveniences are forbidden, church pews in the Mennonite churches are full each Sunday and defections from Mennonite churches are few. In fact, less than a dozen people have left Macon County Mennonite churches in the past twenty years, church leaders say. In the same span, several times as many outsiders (who now make up as much as ten percent of the Mennonite population) have completed months of training sessions and become faithful, productive Mennonites.

Another noticeable change in the Mennonite community was the establishment of two new churches in 1989. Clearview Mennonite Church is a sister church to Montezuma Mennonite Church, the original church that was organized in 1953 and was rapidly running out of seating space. Gospel Light Mennonite Church, which belongs to a different national organization than the two Beachy churches, established a more relaxed doctrine, especially in dress code and education. Gospel Light's school was the first to make a move toward a twelve-grade system rather than the eight-grade system that has been in place for decades.

Still, all three churches share many common bonds, and their business associations easily cross philosophical lines. For instance, Levi Mast, bishop at Gospel Light, is manager of the Mennonite cooperative farm services, and Perry Yoder, head of the Clearview board of education, is his right-hand man.

Members of the same families often attend different churches, and a pair of brothers have been ordained in different churches. Donny Swartzentruber is a minister at Montezuma Mennonite Church and his older brother, Dennis, is a minister at Clearview.

Leaders from all three churches often join forces for such outreach programs as the prison ministry. Also, religious and education leaders from all three churches joined in group interviews for these articles, and they unanimously agreed that they have much more in common than they have differences. Together, they try to hold on to a way of life that was established more than 400 years ago.

Where There's a Need . . .

When a tornado destroyed much of Fort Valley in 1975, some sixty Mennonites showed up to help clean up. Even though residents were still in shock over the utter destruction, they expressed amazement at—and gratitude for—the skill and efficiency of the Mennonites. Until that tornado, the Mennonite Disaster Service, founded in the late 1950s, was something local folks might have seen on the national news, something they never dreamed they would need.

Since then, the Mennonites have shown up in dozens of places, including the site of a devastating tornado in Putnam County several years ago and the Flood of 1994, which paralyzed the midstate for weeks. Preston Williams, mayor of Montezuma, recalled their efforts on behalf of his community this way: "The downtown merchants were about ready to give up until the Mennonites came in. They stuck with us through the entire time (of recovery), always asking if they could do more. That meant a lot to the spirit of this town. And, after all they did here, they went to Oglethorpe and right on down the river all the way to Newton," almost a hundred miles to the south.

The mayor said that while the Flood of '94 will always be the most memorable performance by the Mennonites, it was not the first time the town benefitted from this group. "When the snow storm hit in 1973, they came in with their front-end loaders and opened up the town," he said. "That was the first time they came to our rescue."

The Mennonites also have a reputation for remaining at a disaster scene long after government agencies have gone home. Unlike government agencies, Mennonites never distinguish between public property and private property. "They simply do what needs to be done," Williams said. People often ask who these miracle workers are and where they came from. For the most part, they are farmers, said Lloyd Swartzentruber, head of the local Mennonite Disaster Service and a leader in its sister organization, Christian Aid Ministry. They honed their building skills by erecting their own barns and sheds and, sometimes, their homes. When needed, they come from near and far, Swartzentruber said.

After a disaster strikes, a call goes out by telephone. Mennonites don't watch the evening news because television sets and commercial radios are banned in their community. Those who answer the call leave their farms in the hands of others. Sometimes, several families will pitch in to keep a disaster relief worker's farm operation on schedule.

The Mennonites always seem to muster enough workers to get the job done. Swartzentruber says the workers who showed up in Fort Valley in 1975 came from Pennsylvania, Virginia, North Carolina, Kentucky and Tennessee, and they came to work, bringing their own tools and even some supplies.

When Montezuma was digging out, many out-of-state Mennonites again showed up, but this time, the disaster was very personal to local Mennonites, and they often swelled the ranks of relief workers to 100 or more.

Through it all, Mennonites keep a low profile and they decline to track the hours worked on relief projects, Swartzentruber said. "We specifically avoid it. We do this unto the Lord and, because of that, we work with a lot of enthusiasm.

"We let the Red Cross, National Guard and the others do their job, but they don't come off the sidewalks (and onto private property). We come in later, and we especially look for those victims without insurance, the elderly, the poor. We want to help those who can't help themselves."

However, there is a price that able-bodied disaster victims must pay. They either work shoulder-to-shoulder with the Mennonites or the Mennonites will move on to other endeavors.

No one knows that better than Amanda Edwards, whose jewelry and gift store was swamped in six feet of water during the flood. "I didn't know if I could have faced the day without them telling me what to do," she said. "But I also knew that if I sat down and waited for them to do the work, they would have left. I'd always thought they were unapproachable, but it turned out that they are very normal people. No, I take that back. They are very wonderful people. They must have worked 800-900 hours for me and they did it for nothing."

Besides working long, hard hours, the disaster relief teams are careful with contributed money. "We go in and investigate," Swartzentruber said. "We don't take someone else's word" for what needs to be done.

In addition to disaster relief, Mennonites are deeply involved in an array of other types of mission work. About sixty young Mennonites are working at any given time to help operate a home for brain-injured children in Virginia. Mennonites also operate a nursing home in Arkansas. They show Haitians how to drill wells for fresh water, and they teach farmers in Belgium how to use combines to harvest crops. Sometimes, a project lasts a couple of weeks like those in Haiti. For the young folks in Virginia, it can be a year or more. And some take up mission work strictly as a way of life.

For their work, they surely are blessed, Swartzentruber says. "I made fourteen trips to Haiti in just four years," he said. "And I had better crops in those four years than I can remember having at any other time." With a hearty laugh, he added. "Maybe I need to be gone more."

The Mennonite Church

In Mennonite country, there is no welfare department. No Social Security office. No Medicare. Most Mennonites feel that none is needed. When members of this devoutly religious sect need help, they simply turn to the church. It is the spiritual hub and financial center of any Mennonite community.

In Macon County, three churches—Montezuma Mennonite Church, Clearview and Gospel Light—serve the spiritual and financial needs of about 550 Mennonites. Those services run from religious guidance and support to health insurance and education systems.

In fact, there isn't much the church won't do for members in good standing. To stay in good standing, however, a person must live a righteous and reverent lifestyle, adhering to one of the strictest religious doctrines in the world.

Most outsiders probably would find Mennonite rules much too strict. Although rules may vary somewhat from church to church, the overall doctrine based on eighteen "articles of faith" guide a Mennonite's everyday life. Many things that are a part of everyday life for outsiders are shunned by the Mennonites in Macon County. For example: No television sets of any kind are allowed, and Mennonite children are told not to watch television when they visit a non-Mennonite home or business. Movie attendance is strictly forbidden. Use of illicit drugs, alcoholic beverages or tobacco products is strictly forbidden. Mennonite women do not patronize beauty shops. Night clubs or entertainment centers are off limits to Mennonites. Flashy clothing—and that includes most designer wear—is forbidden. All three Mennonite churches in Macon County enforce dress codes, some more strict than others. Makeup, jewelry, and any kind of glittery accessories are forbidden.

Knowing how the Mennonites live, one Macon County outsider ticked off those forbidden things one by one and then observed, "If I took all of those things out of my life, I'd be a rich man. But I don't think my family could get along without them . . . and neither could I."

However, people who grow up in the Mennonite faith and never have those things surely do not miss them, Mennonite leaders say. Less than ten percent of Mennonite church membership comes from outside the Mennonite community, church leaders say. Surprisingly, the retention rate for outside converts is very high—about 95 percent nationwide.

Donny Swartzentruber, a minister at Montezuma Mennonite Church, said that while seven members of his church—all young people—have been excommunicated in the past twenty years, none was an outsider who had completed training sessions and been baptized. "I think one reason for that," Swartzentruber said, "is that those who came from outside know what the real world is like and they don't want to ever go back."

Another reason for the high retention rate is that wannabes are weeded out during a demanding "training period." A person who wants to join the Mennonite church starts his or her religious journey much like Baptists and other Protestant faiths, starting with a confession of sins and an acceptance of Christ as his or her savior.

Before one can be baptized in the Mennonite faith, however, the convert must attend a dozen or more training sessions in which a church leader will review the eighteen "articles of faith" from the Dortrecht Confession of 1632. Those sessions usually are spread over several months.

Baptism takes place only when church leaders are convinced that the convert has progressed to the point that he or she will adhere strictly to Mennonite doctrine. A Mennonite church is

usually governed by three people: a bishop, a minister and a deacon. Larger churches often have more than one minister.
As a rule, the bishop sets the philosophical pace, the ministers preach the gospel, and the deacon takes care of the church's financial matters. The bishop and deacon take an occasional turn in the pulpit, too.

Interestingly, church leaders are chosen by lot. This "blind-draw" procedure, most Mennonites believe, eliminates the chance that a church leader or group of leaders will choose their successors and thereby establish a dynasty. When a new bishop or minister is needed, three steps are taken. First, the congregation nominates a person or persons by "voices." At a recent nomination service for a bishop at Clearview, fifteen "voices" (oral nominations) were needed. That number can vary, depending on the size of the congregation. (If the "voices" are unanimous, then the selection process ends there.)

Next, there is a period of fasting and praying, both by the candidates and by members of the congregation. Finally, at a Sunday service, a church leader places a card in one of several song books (the number of books corresponding to the number of candidates). After several shuffling processes by different church leaders, each of the candidates picks a book from a table at the front of the sanctuary. The candidate holding the book containing the card is the "chosen" one.

10

MILITARY LIFE

Since I spent twenty years in the uniform of a United States Marine, you know I have plenty to say about the military. In twenty-five years of writing for newspapers, I tried to document some of the heroes, some of the stories, some of the lessons that I gathered during my other career. I wrote about those things because I wanted future generations—perhaps generations that will never have to hear a shot fired in war—to know the kind of people we were and the kind of lives we led.

Cecil A. Britt
An American Hero
(from a column published on October 27, 1995)

We need heroes. All of us. I'm not talking about the Power Rangers here. Nor my old cowboy heroes like Gene Autry and the Sunset Kid. No, I'm talking about people who made great sacrifices for us all, those who put their lives on the line time after time. Such a hero is Cecil A. Britt, who lives quietly in the south end of Macon, helps his wife grow beautiful flowers, and turns planks into Christmas reindeer for wide-eyed youngsters.

Cecil will turn seventy-five next July, and I'll bet that even people who know him are unaware of what he did for our country. This old soldier earned *seven* Purple Hearts. That isn't a record, I know. But it has not happened since World War II, and I doubt that it will ever happen again.

Anyone who was wounded three times in Vietnam would almost certainly never have seen a battlefield again. In Cecil's day, the Purple Heart was no big deal. The attitude was: Just keep fighting, soldier, we'll total up the medals after the war.

He grew up in Griffin and his father was killed when Cecil was just two, so Cecil and his six brothers and sisters learned self-reliance at an early age by helping earn a living and bearing personal responsibility. When he graduated, Cecil, an all-around athlete, went to Columbus and played professional baseball. But there wasn't much money in minor league baseball. Besides, that line of work was much too seasonal.

A sergeant who saw him play at nearby Fort Benning told the young athlete that he could play baseball and get a regular paycheck in the Army. So Cecil enlisted, and for several years, he was among the Army's finest athletes, playing baseball and football, and doing some boxing, too. Cecil was good enough in the ring that the Army once sent him all the way to Hawaii to fight the Navy's welterweight champ. Cecil won on a third-round knockout.

The next time Cecil saw Hawaii was on December 6, 1941. He disembarked the day before Pearl Harbor was bombed. Cecil was not wounded in that attack, but he helped patch up the wounded. Then he went to war.

As an infantryman with the 11th Airborne Division, Cecil saw the Pacific fighting at close range. He hopped from island to island, always parachuting into combat. He spent more than eleven months on the front lines, in the foxholes, dodging bullets. He was wounded the first two times at Leyte, a small island in the Philippines. But he says, "My wounds were not very serious. I never missed a jump." During the fighting there, Cecil was awarded a battlefield commission by General Douglas MacArthur.

Later, on the island of Luzon, Cecil and three other Americans were captured, and he says Japanese troops "just lined us up and shot us." He was wounded only in the leg and survived; the others did not. His fellow soldiers found him about eight hours later. A stomach wound in 1943 took him out of action for a while, and he was given a chance to go home.

Back in Georgia, he married Evelyn Smith of Thomaston, a coworker of one of his sisters, and then he went back to war. That was his only break in nearly six years in the Pacific. By the end of the war, he not only had accumulated the seven Purple Hearts, but he had been awarded both the Silver Star Medal and the Bronze Star Medal, this nation's third- and fourth-highest awards for valor in combat.

Cecil Britt spent twenty years in the Army and rose to the rank of lieutenant colonel. Then he worked as a civil servant for fifteen more years.

Now, I don't want him and his comrades to be forgotten. His service to this country is important to all of us and, even though he is a reluctant hero, I wanted to put his story in writing . . . lest we forget.

Doc Lowery
A Special Corpsman

(from a column published on September 10, 1990)

A television camera slowly panned across the faces of Marines in Saudi Arabia. Young, determined, steady-eyed. Then I saw the corpsman. Knowing he was there gave me a good feeling. You shouldn't believe all that malarkey about how Marines and sailors don't get along. We've *always* gotten along with our corpsmen.

Although the corpsmen spend most of a career giving shots and handing out aspirin, they've turned out to be some of the bravest souls in combat. Besides that, they'll eat the same food, go to the same hell holes—without a rifle—and still not complain half as much as a Marine.

That newscast jogged my memory about my all-time favorite corpsman—Doc Lowery. Doc and I crossed paths a couple of times, once at Camp Lejeune in the early 1960s and again in West Palm Beach, Florida, in the late 1960s.

Even among corpsmen, Doc Lowery was a jewel. He was surely the best pool shooter I've ever known. I watched him as he ran seventy-five balls in straight pool. I had never seen it done before, and I haven't seen it done since. He also was a tough competitor on the golf course. Although he carried a 6-handicap, he didn't hesitate to play with the best. "I'll double up and get even on the last hole," he'd say. And he usually did. He was as tough under pressure as anyone I've known. He used to say, "Shoot, I'd play Arnold Palmer one hole for the house, car and old lady . . . although I don't know what I'd ever do with two cars, two houses, and two old ladies." Yes, sir, put the money on the line, and I would've bet on Doc every time.

Still, Doc's greatest gift was persuasiveness. He could have talked a miser out of his last glittering gold piece.

He also was a perfect gentleman. He never used profanity in the presence of a woman, and he treated every one of them like a lady.

But Doc's greatest triumph in smoothing things over came following a wreck in 1968. He and another member of our staff in West Palm Beach had gone to Homestead Air Force Base, south of Miami, to pick up supplies. On the way back, Doc, who opted to drive his brand-new car on the trip instead of a military vehicle, failed to negotiate a curve on a cloverleaf overpass and crashed through a guardrail.

His passenger that day—a guy who had the demeanor of an undertaker—later told us how the car rolled over three times down a long embankment and came to rest on its wheels. Both passenger and driver escaped with only bumps and bruises. When the policeman showed up, Doc was most helpful. He even held one end of the tape while the officer took measurements. Finally, the officer put his clipboard on the wrinkled hood of Doc's car, and with Doc's driver's license in hand, began writing.

Looking over the officer's shoulder, Doc was surprised to see that he was writing a ticket. The reported conversation went something like this:

"Ahem! Excuse me, officer, but may I ask what you're doing?"

"Writing you a citation."

"Writing a citation? For me? And why in the *world* would you write *me* a citation?"

"For failing to have your car under control."

Doc never hesitated. He gestured back toward the top of the embankment and said, "Officer, I'd like to make a point. Look up there. I want you to notice that I came through that guard-rail and didn't even knock down one of your posts. I rolled that car over *three* times and brought it back on its wheels. Then my passenger and I climbed out without a scratch."

He put on a pained expression and added, "And you don't think I had control of my car?"

The officer stared in disbelief, then he smiled, then he broke up with laughter. "Wait till the guys at the station hear this one," he said.

Doc retrieved his driver's license and never did get a ticket.

Watching that newscast the other night, I was thinking that perhaps we need Doc in Saudi Arabia, not as a corpsman but as a mediator. Yes, sir, I wonder what Saddam Hussein would think of my pal, Doc Lowery. . . .

(Incidentally, Doc Lowery was the youngest chief in the Navy in 1945 at age nineteen, and, after a ten-year absence, he returned as the oldest seaman in the Navy. He also wore a chest full of medals, including the Silver Star. He was a hero. Last I heard of him, he was living in Texas.)

Burning Love
(from a column first published in 1979)

She paused when I stopped and asked directions. And while she was directing me, I noticed the bundles of letters in her small, time-worn hands.

"Lots of mail today?" I asked.

She smiled and said, "No, they're old—very old—love letters."

"Oh?"

"Yes, I'm going to burn them."

"Really?"

"Yes. They're from Harry. My husband . . . my late husband."

"Old love letters, huh?"

"Yes, very old. World War I."

"That was a long time ago."

"Yes, I was very young then. And he was very handsome. We met on this street. He was attending Mercer University. He quit school to join the Army."

"People don't quit college anymore to fight wars. They stay in college to keep from fighting wars."

"Yes, I know. But my Harry wasn't like that."

"He wanted to go?"

"Yes, he said all of his friends were already there. . ."

"And he just had to go?"

"Yes, he caught a train right down there, and he went away."

"But he wrote a lot of letters?"

"Yes, so many of them. . ."

"And now you're going to burn them?"

"Yes, they say too many things . . . too many intimate things."

"And that's bad?"

"No, I didn't say that. I just wouldn't want anyone else to ever read them."

"Not *anyone?*"

"Not even my own children."

"That intimate, huh?"

"Yes, I started reading one . . . and I think I blushed!"

"Harry wrote something like *that?*"

"Yes, he was very lonely over there. He told me about himself, how he felt about . . . everything."

"And it made you blush?"

"Well, yes. He said some things . . . some very personal things."

"Did Harry keep your letters?"

"Oh, no! There's no way he could have kept all of my letters. I wrote every day."

"*Every* day?"

"Yes, Harry said my letters made the next day worth living as he was fighting through France."

"France. That's some place to be fighting a war."

"Yes, we went over there years later. Harry showed me some of the places where he fought. But it didn't look like there had ever been a war—unless you looked for bullet marks on the older houses and buildings."

She paused and then asked, "Are you married?"

"Yes."

"Did you ever go to war?"

"Vietnam."

"And did you write love letters to your wife?"

"I tried. But I wasn't very good at it."

"Does she still have them?"

"I don't know."

"Did you ever write anything that would make her blush?"

"Probably . . . yes."

"If she still has them, what do you think she will do with them someday?"

"Probably burn them."

"Is that what you would want her to do?"

"I don't know. I never thought about it before."

"I didn't think about it until I read that first letter . . . after all those years."

"And you're really going to burn them?"

"Yes. I think it's time."

"And you think Harry would approve?"

"Yes. . . I think so . . ."

Then she walked away, her steps short and slow. She stopped at a drum with rusty sides and soot around the top that had been left from other fires.

The fire already was burning. She began dropping the letters into the drum, one by one. She never once looked back at me. I stood watching her for a little longer. And I wonder if Marvalene would make a trip to a steel drum someday and burn a lot of old memories.

Willie Lee Duckworth
His Words Made the Army March
(from a column published on September 17, 1989)

Ain't no use in goin' home
Jody's got your gal and gone
Ain't no use in feelin' blue
Jody's got your sister, too
Sound off (one, two)
Sound off . . . .

In forty-five years, millions of soldiers have chanted those words and dozens of similar verses as they marched and double-timed the endless miles. They surely will be chanting those verses a hundred years from now. Because there will be cadence as long as there are soldiers, Willie Lee Duckworth of Sandersville has attained a certain immortality for writing "Sound Off." It also earned him some money—enough to buy his own pulpwood truck and open his own business.

But he has received little recognition outside his hometown. He says that doesn't bother him, but I think that, deep inside, it has to.

Willie Lee Duckworth was born in Washington County sixty-five years ago. He quit high school to try farming, and then at nineteen he was drafted and shipped off to Fort Slocum in New York. That's where he left an indelible mark on Army cadence.

Since even the services practiced segregation in those days, blacks and whites seldom drilled together. When nine black soldiers at Fort Slocum had a hard time drilling to the commands of a white officer, Mr. Duckworth, then a buck private, was told to drill the blacks.

The Georgian made up the words that day as he went along. Very shortly, white soldiers took up the chants, too. Colonel Bernard Lentz, the base commander, heard the chant and soon ordered its use by all soldiers.

With twenty-three verses furnished by Duckworth and the help of base musicians, the colonel put it to music and published it in a cadence manual. At the time, the cadence was "The Duckworth Chant."

After the war, Duckworth returned to Sandersville and worked in a sawmill until the early 1950s when his chant became a hit song with the title "Sound Off." It was performed by Vaughn Monroe. It also became the basis of a movie by that name, and Mickey Rooney had the starring role. Since then, parts of "Sound Off" have been used in dozens of movies, including "Private Benjamin." Each time it is used, Duckworth gets a royalty check.

When the movie "Sound Off" was going well, Duckworth said he received as much as $1,000 per month—certainly a pretty fair sum in the 1950s. But he didn't splurge with the money. He bought a pulpwood truck and opened his own business. And although the company has remained small and the royalty checks never were that big again, Duckworth and Edna, his wife of forty-five years have lived comfortably and reared six children.

But he always has worked. Still does. One recent day, I had to wait for him to come out of the pine forests to be interviewed. The man I met is tall, slender and likeable. He's also very frank about "Sound Off" and how it has affected his life. He talked about:

- Recognition—"I've never had much, but it doesn't bother me like it might bother some people. I'd rather be out fishing than anything you can name."

- The movie world—"I've never met Mickey Rooney or Goldie Hawn. I'd like to meet them, but it doesn't bother me that I haven't."

- The immortality of his chant—"It makes me feel good that someone might still be using it a hundred years from now. I just wish I was gonna be here to hear it."

- Changes in his work—Many verses have been added and someone changed the name in the original version from Jody to Alvin when it was published. "But that doesn't bother me, either—as long as they keep sending the checks."

Well, Willie Lee Duckworth may never have made it in big-time entertainment, but the folks who run Washington County's Kaolin Festival plan to treat him like a celebrity. The festival theme is "Washington County Sounds Off," and Mr. Duckworth is going to be grand marshal of the parade, the first black person ever to be so honored.

But as soon as the festival is over, I'm betting he goes fishing. To him, snaring a big-mouth bass is better than hobnobbing any day.

Happy Birthday, Marines
(from a column published on November 10, 1986)

Today is the much-celebrated birthday of the U.S. Marine Corps, and, to help celebrate, I'd like to tell you about a character who made sure I never forgot him. He was known as Staff Sergeant Tallbear. If he had a first name, I never heard it. He was my drill instructor during the first few weeks I spent in boot camp.

From the beginning, he obviously didn't think much of my 132 pounds on a six-foot frame. I sweated bullets the first time I ever saw him, and he wasted no time in letting me know that he didn't think a scrawny eighteen-year-old like me could ever be a Marine. "My name," he said in his welcoming speech as he held a gleaming sword in his right hand, "is Staff Sergeant Tallbear. I am a full-blooded Cherokee Indian and I am not tame. For the next ten weeks, I am going to be your mother, your father, your sister and your brother. But the first one of you maggots who mistakes me for your girlfriend. . . ."

Well, I'd better censor his speech right there. I'm sure you understand that he said some words that will never appear in a family newspaper. But foul language, meanness and all, he was both a teacher and a hero to me. When he was wearing his dress uniform, a dozen ribbons decorated his chest.

"All of these ribbons except one came from service in Korea," he told us that first day. "The other one was pinned on me because I cut off more arms with this sword than any other drill instructor in the history of the United States Marine Corps!" He almost always carried that sword, so I kept my arms very close to my sides. Which is exactly where he wanted them, I'm sure.

I once made the mistake of thinking we might become friends. After all, I had learned that he hailed from Oklahoma, too. When he asked about my home state, I smiled from ear to ear and said, "Oklahoma, sir!"

He walked up very close to me and suddenly socked me in the gut. As I gulped for air, he leaned down close to my ear and said, "You don't know about me, do you, you low-life maggot?"

I couldn't even shake my head in the negative. All I could do was gulp for air. "Well, I was *run out* of Oklahoma, you (bleep)-head. I wanted to kill everything in Oklahoma!" He smiled with pearly white teeth and added, "But being here, I don't have to go back there to kill Okies. They're sending them to me!" When I could finally straighten up, he whopped me again.

He gave me many reasons to hate him. Because we weren't very good at marching during that first week, he decided to improve our teamwork by having us sweep the asphalt parade field—with toothbrushes. I never knew there could be so much dirt on one little part of a parade field.

He thumped me again a few times, and I made a promise to myself that I would scatter those pearly white teeth all over the parade field as soon as I graduated.

Then Staff Sergeant Tallbear taught me an unforgettable lesson at the obstacle course. (I was reminded of this in a movie years later, but I *lived* it.)

There was a wall on the obstacle course that stood maybe ten feet high. It looked more like fifty. The first time we attempted the course, I hit the wall like a sack of feed. I fell backward, stunned by the collision. Before I could scramble to my feet, he was standing over me. "Get off your (bleep), maggot, and try again."

I did. I failed again. "Get up and try again, maggot."

After half a dozen failed attempts, I could only lie there and wonder if I could physically rise again. The DI stood up against the sky and pointed his sword down at me. "Boyd, you wouldn't make a pimple on a real Marine's fanny. Do you know that? I wouldn't want you on my side in combat. You'd get my (bleep) shot off. So I'm going to get you a girlie discharge from my Marine Corps. Like I said, Boyd, you wouldn't make a pimple. . . ."

Before he could finish, I was up. I didn't know whether I was going to hit him or the wall. The wall didn't have a sword. I hit it again. This time, my hands reached higher than ever, my feet clawed against the boards, and somehow I went over the top.

He was already on the other side of the wall. "Try again, Boyd. You got lucky. You can't do it twice." I did it three times. No sweat. After that day, boot camp was . . . well, it wasn't a picnic, but it was tolerable.

Staff Sergeant Tallbear switched to another platoon when we were about halfway through training, but he came back for the graduation. The other guys shook his hand. I did, too.

The DI looked at my 180 pounds and said, "Boyd, I would have bet the outhouse that you wouldn't make it."

But I had.

If I ever think I can't get up and go at it again, I suppose I'll see that sword gleaming in the sunlight and I'll hear that voice. And I'll get up. I know I will.

Happy birthday, Marines.

11

CLASSIC HUMOR: SOMETHING OLD, SOMETHING BORROWED . . .

*J*oe Parham, long-time editor of the Macon News who wrote more than 5,000 columns before his death in 1980, was one of the greatest writers I ever knew. He also admitted that he sometimes "borrowed" from other writers. Like the classic yarn in this chapter about the mule with a bugle stuck in its south end. But Joe offered an explanation for borrowing tales from other writers: "If you steal from one person," Joe said, "that's plagiarism. But if you steal from lots of people, that's called research!" Just want you folks to know that a lot of "research" went into this chapter. Some of the stories are my own; some are borrowed. But they are here for one reason—your enjoyment.

Sounding the Trumpet

One fine Carolina evening, a Mrs. George (Fannie Lamb) Wood, now deceased, called a Dr. Marvin Satterfield of Edenton from her home in Chowan County. It was about her mule Horace. She was upset and said, "Doctor, Horace is sick, and I wish you'd come out and take a look." Dr. Satterfield said, "Oh, Fannie Lamb, it's after six o'clock and I'm eating supper. Just give him a good dose of mineral oil, and if he isn't all right in the morning, phone me and I'll come out."

She wanted to know how to give the mule the mineral oil, and the doctor said it should be given through a funnel. Mrs. Wood protested that the mule might bite her, and Dr. Satterfield, a bit exasperated, said: "You're a farm woman and you know about these things, Fannie Lamb. Give it to him in the other end. "

So Fannie Lamb went out to the barn, and there stood Horace, his head held down and just a-moaning and a-groaning. She looked around for a funnel, but the nearest thing she could find was her Uncle Bill's fox hunting horn hanging on the wall, a beautiful gold-plated instrument with silver tassels hanging from it. She took down the horn and nervously affixed it properly. Horace paid no attention, and she was encouraged.

Then she reached up on the shelf where the medicines for farm animals were kept. But instead of picking up the mineral oil, she picked up a bottle of turpentine. And she poured a liberal dose into the horn.

Horace raised his head with a sudden jerk and stood dead still for maybe three seconds. Then he let out a squeal that could be heard a mile down the road, reared up on his hind legs, brought down his front legs and kicked out one side of the barn, jumped a five-foot fence and started down the road at a mad gallop.

Because Horace was in pain, the horn would blow every time he jumped. All of the dogs in the neighborhood knew that when the horn was blowing, Uncle Bill was going fox hunting. So out on the road they went, following close behind Horace.

People who witnessed that chase said it was an unforgettable sight. First, Horace running at top speed, the horn in a most-unusual position, mellow notes issuing therefrom, tassels waving and dogs barking joyously.

They passed the home of Old Man Harvey Hogan, who was sitting on his front porch. It was said that he hadn't drawn a sober breath in fifteen years. He gazed in fascinated amazement at the sight that unfolded before his eyes. He couldn't believe what he was seeing. (Incidentally, he is now head man in Alcoholics Anonymous in the Albemarle section of the state.)

By this time, it was good and dark. Horace and the dogs were approaching the inland waterway, and the bridge tender heard the horn blowing frantically. He figured a fast boat was approaching, so he hurriedly cranked the bridge up. Horace went overboard and was drowned. The dogs also went into the water, but they swam out.

Now it so happens that the bridge tender was running for the office of sheriff in Chowan County, but he managed to poll just seven votes.

People figured that any man who didn't know the difference between a mule with a horn up its caboose and a boat coming down the inland waterway certainly wasn't fit to hold any public office in Chowan County.

Well-Dressed Bird

In winter, when a splash of color was seldom seen on an Oklahoma farm, the parrot came to live with us. That colorful bird just magically appeared one day amid the panorama of a weather-beaten, unpainted house, a barn that also was unpainted and fields where absolutely nothing grew at that time of year.

In a couple of months, spring would bring green grass and Mama would surely take her colorful quilts outdoors, hang them on the clothesline and beat the winter's dust from them. But the sight of the colorful parrot made us forget the drab landscape of winter.

Mama saw the bird first. It was eating among the chickens. It would use its considerable beak to bump any daring chickens out of the way and then gobble up whatever was there to eat. "Oh, that's a pretty bird," Mama said. "And look at the blue tail feather. Wouldn't that look good on my Sunday-go-to-meetin' hat?"

But Mama would never have hurt a bird by yanking out a tail feather. She was much too kind-hearted. Mama did try to lure the bird indoors. However, none of her ploys worked. Even food in the hand would not let her make friends with the parrot. In fact, it showed a distinct dislike for every living creature, man or beast. It seemed to be happiest when it was robbing the chickens of their dinner. My goodness, that bird could eat—anything and everything and in vast quantities.

Our preacher, the Reverend Providence Story, came to visit soon after the bird arrived. He squinted his bushy eyebrows and gazed at the creature, and he began telling Mama that parrots lived longer than almost any other animal in the world. "It's not unusual," he said, "for parrots to live a hundred years or more."

He seemed to know a lot about parrots, but he couldn't get close enough to that parrot to make a guess on its age.

Several days after Mama first spotted the parrot in our yard, she also discovered that some of the strawberries she had canned back in June had spoiled. She said the seals on the fruit jars didn't do the job. So she emptied the spoiled strawberries into a pan and then washed the jars and put them away for next summer's harvest. But she didn't throw away the strawberries. They sat there and sat there, and, finally, the kids started complaining. "Throw out the strawberries, Mama. They're spoiled."

She told us not to get rambunctious, that she had to guard the food supply—even for the chickens—through the winter. She would feed them to the chickens in her own good time, she said, and they stayed on a side table for several more days.

Finally, Mama threw out the spoiled fruit. What we didn't know was that, while making bread, Mama had spilled some lard into the pan of strawberries. I guess you know what lard did to the spoiled fruit. We had some 100-proof strawberries on our hands and didn't even know it! When Mama threw them out in the yard, here came that gluttonous parrot, bumping hens with its beak and gobbling up those strawberries, a parrot making a pig of itself.

The next morning Mama looked out the window and saw the parrot lying in the yard. It wasn't moving. Mama thought the bird was dead. She was very sad. "I guess that bird had lived out its hundred years," she said. And she went out in the yard and carried the carcass up to the table on the back porch.

"I might as well have that blue feather for my Sunday-go-to-meetin' hat," she said, and she plucked that feather.

Suddenly, she was surrounded by noisy kids, jumping up and down and saying things like, "Oh, Mama, make me one of those

Indian headdresses." We proceeded to pluck every feather off the parrot. Finally, Mama handed the carcass to Curtis and me and said, "Y'all take it out and bury it."

Well, sir, there wasn't any way we were going to dig a grave for that bird. We just threw it down in a draw and went back to the house. The next morning, Mama looked out the window to see that parrot—hung over and buck naked—standing out in the yard just a-shiverin'. That sight broke Mama's tender heart. "Oh, what have we done," she wailed.

Curtis and I caught the critter. Him being still three sheets to the wind, that wasn't hard to do. We brought him back onto the porch, wrapped a dish rag around his bare body and tried to decide what to do.

One thing we found out for sure: You can't put feathers back on a bird. The kids tried, but it just couldn't be done. So we could keep our Indian headdresses, but what about the bird?

Mama, bless her thoughtful ways, decided to make some clothes for the parrot. She got out her needles and knitted it a little red sweater. Then she used some scraps of cloth to make him a little pair of overalls. While he was still hung over, we put the clothes on him and turned him a-loose.

I'm here to tell that we still don't know how long that parrot will live. Last time I was out in Oklahoma, I saw him struttin' down the street in a pair of Calvin Klein jeans and shirt with a little alligator on the pocket!

Zipper Lore

(from a column first published in 1986)

A classic story is making the rounds these days, and this is my slightly embellished version. A young couple was having the first really serious argument since their wedding. What caused the disagreement isn't important. It was the Mexican standoff that mattered. After bitter words, she stomped away to sleep in the guest room; he collapsed on that lonely couch many husbands know so well.

Cold silence dominated the breakfast table the next morning as each waited for the other to admit being wrong and apologize. It didn't happen. Finally, she left the table, her feet stomping another noisy tattoo through the house as she went to get dressed. She picked out her favorite dress and, when she couldn't get it zipped up in back without help, she grudgingly went to her mate.

She didn't speak to him. She glared at him and then turned around and gestured toward the zipper she couldn't reach. The angry husband saw a chance to strike a vengeful blow. "She wants me to zip her up?" he thought. "I'll do a zipper job she'll never forget."

He quickly ran the zipper to the top, but, before she could step out of his reach, he just as quickly zipped it back down. She glared at him, turned the zipper his way again and gestured. Still, not a word had been spoken. This time, he gave one quick jerk toward the top, but, before he reached the top, he jerked it downward. He repeated the maneuver several times. Finally, the zipper broke.

The wife bit her lip to keep from really blowing her top. She hurriedly changed into another dress that buttoned up the front and left the house without even looking at her husband. She seethed all day.

By the time she arrived home late in the afternoon, she'd vowed to get revenge for the broken zipper. She must do that, she told herself, before they could ever settle the original spat. But she never expected to be afforded such a golden opportunity as that which she saw when she arrived home. As she walked through the garage, she saw two legs, clad in the work clothes of her husband, sticking out from under his car. She smiled wickedly and hunkered down beside those legs. She reached for his zipper and yanked it down. It didn't break. She yanked it back up and back down and back up and back down. It still didn't break. Angrily, she grabbed a part of his fly in each hand and pulled as hard as she could in opposite directions. At last, the zipper broke. That, by golly, evened a score.

Glowing with satisfaction, she strode into the kitchen. And there, seated at the table and sipping a cup of coffee, was her husband. "Oh, my God!"she said. "What have I done?"

She explained what had just happened in the garage. His buddy from his job was working under the car, he told her. For the moment, they put their differences aside and went to the garage to offer an explanation.

In the garage, they called the friend's name. No answer. They called again. No answer. Frantically, they pulled the other man from beneath the car. He was unconscious, and he was bleeding from a nasty gash across his forehead. He had tried several times to sit up during the assault on his zipper by the angry wife.

With a wet washcloth and some cheek-patting, they revived him. Then they helped him into a car and took him to the hospital. The cut required only half a dozen stitches. Last I heard, the friend had recovered but vowed to never work beneath a car again.

And the young couple? They're still together. He calls her Zippy and she calls him . . . well, whatever comes to mind.

"Ain't Nothing the Same Anymore"
(from a column published on June 22, 1992)

A couple of my friends were talking the other day about how some good things had been lost from "the old days." They talked about marbles and mumblety-peg, old Hudsons and passenger trains, scrub-boards and eight-day clocks. They rambled on for a while, and finally, they asked me what I remembered. So I told them about a trip I took last summer with Wonderful Wanda, my foster daughter, back to the Oklahoma town where the old man grew up.

After my daddy died, I told her, we moved off that sharecropper's farm. I was tired of being poor, so I shined shoes on a street corner, caddied at the golf course, set pins at the bowling alley. Those were jobs that helped me grow up, but they are also kid's jobs that disappeared with this so-called progress.

I told her about living in an upstairs apartment with the first electric lights and indoor plumbing my family could actually call "ours." Back then, there were no suburbs. Most city folks lived close to the business section of town, and some of us lived in second-floor apartments in downtown buildings.

You could tell who had money back then by where they lived. People with good incomes lived over businesses like dry-goods stores that closed at 5:30. With the stores empty, there was nothing but peace and quiet for those who lived upstairs.

We didn't have a lot of money, so we lived over a juke joint. Did you ever hear a bunch of drunks trying to harmonize "Peace in the Valley" with Red Foley at about midnight on Saturday? It was enough to send me to the Baptist church on Sunday morning to hear a good choir.

The building that once was a juke joint was gone when we went back. A bank parking lot had replaced my house of memories. And the junkyard across the street where we played cowboys and Indians. . . . What had happened to it? Oh, yeah, I forgot. Junkyards aren't allowed in the city anymore.

So where do kids find an old Hudson or Terraplane to use as a mountain or a secret hideout? Simple, I told Wanda, kids don't play cowboys and Indians anymore. They watch television and get fat from eating potato chips and guzzling soda pop for breakfast.

Well, there was still the Baptist Church, I told her. Yes, sir, that's where I learned to talk to Jesus. Baccalaureate services were held there when I graduated from high school. But the old church with the huge sandstone pillars was gone. A parking lot had replaced it, too. The new, modern, brick church building was across the street. It was round. Cute, but where's the front door?

Well, c'mon uptown, I told her. Let me show you where I learned to shoot pool with one eye on the cue ball and one on the door, watching for Daddy Philpot. He was the best step-daddy a boy ever had, but he never tolerated his young'uns hanging around some smoke-choked pool hall. Gone. A clerk at a hardware store across the street said it burned down years ago. I thought about Mama. She used to pray right out loud, "Lord, if you don't burn that place down, I'm going to." I guess the Lord finally heard her.

"Everything's changed," I told Wanda. "Even the coyotes are on welfare." She didn't understand, so I explained it to her. When I was a kid, coyotes used to team up, three or four of them chasing a long-legged jackrabbit. They'd catch it and kill it and eat it. By working together, coyotes survived.

Know what those suckers are doing now? They're sitting beside Interstate 40, waiting for an 18-wheeler to kill their dinner for them! That's coyotes on welfare.

I looked at the two guys who'd started this conversation and very solemnly said, "Yes, sir, ain't nothing the same anymore. . . ."

Poor Old Blue
(from a column first published in 1981)

I won't often bore you with a dog story, but. . . . A south Georgia farmer wanted his only son to be a doctor, and, when the boy graduated from high school, the old man took him to the University of Georgia, enrolled him and paid all of the bills. Then the old man really showed his love. He gave the boy his old pickup and $500 spending money to see him through the first quarter.

But, no sooner was the old man out of sight than the kid's roommate introduced him to UGA night life—beer joints and long-haired girls. To say the least, the kid went a little wild. He spent money like it might catch fire at any minute. In two weeks, he was broke. He decided to write for more money.

His roommate, a third-year student who knew the ropes, told him, "Don't use the old stories. Think of something new and different." So the boy from south Georgia thought about Old Blue, the hunting dog that was both a source of family pride and a legend among hunting dogs down that way. And he sat down and wrote:

"Dear Dad: I met the most interesting professor. He's an expert with animals, and when I told him how smart Old Blue is, he said he'd like to try to teach him to count. But it's expensive. He said it would cost $500. But I wanted you to know."

Two days later, Old Blue arrived special delivery accompanied by $500 and a note saying that "nothing is too good for Old Blue." The kid tied Old Blue to the clothesline, gave him some food and headed out to happy hour.

Two weeks later, the kid was in financial straits again. But his innovative spirit was just beginning to sprout. He fired off another letter:

"Dear Dad: Old Blue's progress is remarkable. The professor said he's the smartest dog in the world. The professor says he thinks he can teach him how to read, but it will cost $1,000. I know it's a lot of money, but I wanted you to know."

A couple of days later, the $1,000 arrived. Old Blue got another supply of dog food, and the kid hit the beer joints again. The money lasted three weeks. Then the kid wrote again.

"Dear Dad: Well, Old Blue has really done it. He's learned how to count. He's learned how to read. And now the professor says he thinks he can teach him to talk. But it will cost another $1,000. I know it's a lot of money, but I wanted you to know."

Naturally, the old man sent another thousand. Old Blue got more dog food and the kid returned to his wild and wooly ways. The new money got him through the quarter, but, as he headed home for a visit with Old Blue riding in the seat beside him, he knew he couldn't take the dog home with him. So he pulled to the side of a country highway, got his .22 rifle (all country boys own a rifle) and called Old Blue out of the truck.

"Sorry, old fellow," he said, as he put a bullet between Old Blue's eyes. Then he buried the dog in a cotton patch and drove on home.

The old man hurried into the front yard when the kid drove up and welcomed him. Then he looked around and asked, "Where's Old Blue?"

"Well, Dad," the kid said, "there's a sad story about Old Blue. Y'see, we were a-comin' home, both of us better educated, of course. Old Blue was counting telephone poles. He must have counted a thousand. When he got bored with that, he read the newspaper to me. And when he finished that, he started talking. And, Dad, the first words out of his mouth were: 'Sure will be good to see the old man. I sure have missed him. But, hey, I wonder if he's still messing around with that widow lady down on River Road?'"

The old man grabbed his son's arm frantically and said, "Why, that big-mouth dog. I hope you shot the son-of-a-gun."

The kid said. "Yes, sir, I did. Right 'tween the eyes."

This Dog Will Hunt!
(from a column first published in 1979)

There are some tall-tale tellers around here. Some folks might tell you that I'm one of them, but that ain't so. Being a newspaper reporter and all, I have to stick pretty much to the facts. Georgia's storytellers especially like to talk about hunting dogs. Like the one about the bird dog that could allegedly walk on water. Listen.

A rich fella from Atlanta went to south Georgia in search of "the best bird dog that ever was." He found what he was looking for on a farm near where my countrified pal Muley grew up. Muley's neighbor, Stump Waters, was known for raising and training good bird dogs. When the city fella showed up down thataway, Stump was quick to tell him that he'd come to the right place. "I've got exactly the dog you're looking for," he told the city fella, but he ain't cheap. He'll cost you $2,500." Stump later told folks that the man from Hotlanta almost fractured a finger or two trying to get a big roll of bills out of his pocket.

After paying for the dog, Stump explained a few things. "Some people don't know how to treat a dog, and it'll stop hunting. Now I want you to try out this dog before you leave, because, once you're gone, I ain't listening to any complaints." So Stump loaned the city fella a shotgun and sent him out to hunt in the nearby fields.

The first time they scared up a bird, the man shot it and it fell in a pond that was Muley's boyhood fishing hole. Would you believe what that bird dog did? It *walked* right across the water, picked up that bird, walked back across the water and dropped it at the hunter's feet. Of course, the hunter was stunned, amazed, and just plain bumfuzzled. "I can't believe this!" he said. "But I've gotta see it again. C'mon, doggie, let's find

CLASSIC HUMOR • 223

another bird." They did, the man shot it over the water, and the dog went after it, still walking across the water in both directions.

The man was hugging the dog and just about in tears with joy when Muley came walking out of the woods with a pole on his shoulder, a bait can in his hand, and visions of catching his dinner dancing in his head.

The city fella grabbed Muley by the arm and said, "Son, I want you to see something. I want you to see this dog hunt!" Being a cooperative soul, Muley went along with the man and the dog. Sure enough, up jumped a bird and the man shot it. And what do you think the dog did? It *walked* right out across the water, picked up that bird, walked back across the water and dropped it at that fella's feet.

By that time, the excited city fella had Muley by the arm and was literally shaking that boy. "Did you see that?" he cried. "Did you see that?"

"Yep," Muley said, "I surely did see it."

"Well, what do you think?"

Muley scrooched up his face and said, "Well, I hate to be the one to tell you, mister, but I think you've been had."

"You think I've been *had*? What do you mean by that?"

"Mister, someone has done sold you a bird dog *that can't swim!*"

Grandma and the Flasher
(from a column first published in 1979)

She's really just a grandmother with Clairol covering the gray. But she certainly knows how to handle a flasher. You know what a flasher is. A person who exposes himself—or herself, I guess—to someone in public. That's a pretty loose definition, but this is a pretty loose column subject.

Anyhow, Grandma was fishing from the dock near her lake home one day, just enjoying the warm sunshine. You know how that feels to old bones and rheumatism. Elderly folks have enough problems just trying to catch their dinner on a hook without some smart aleck zipping past in a boat, stirring up the water and chasing the fish away.

But Grandma had other problems. This boat was pulling a splasher, a nut on water skis. After almost drowning our heroine in a sheet of water, he skimmed back out across the lake. Grandma was dripping wet and cussing mad. She shook her fist at him. He laughed.

Stomping up to her cottage, Grandma got out her binoculars and began scanning the lake for the offending boat. It took a while, but she spotted it, and the skier was in the water. As he crawled into the boat, Grandma hollered indignantly at the boat driver. The skier answered. She got flashed. Just to make sure you understand, this guy pulled his bathing suit down and "mooned" Grandma with his bare behind.

Talk about a mad grandma. She quickly scanned the boat for a number. She found it, and then she called the game warden. The man in green wasn't amused. He located the boat in short order, hauled in the two young men and called Grandma. Lock 'em up, she said, for indecent exposure. The game warden kept the flasher for his parents because he was just sixteen.

His parents rescued the lad from the hoosegow, but Grandma wasn't finished, not by a long shot. Either a full apology is forthcoming or she presses charges, she said. The little game was over. She wasn't going to be a nice old girl. Not after being flashed, anyhow.

It wasn't long, she later recalled, before three people came walking up to her dock. One man, one woman, one teenage boy. In her words, all three were "scrubbed church-going clean." The adults spoke. They were there to hear their son apologize for his short-lived career as a flasher. But, before the boy could offer the apology that they hoped would end the affair, Grandma spoke:

"From the actions of your son, I take it there is something special about his posterior. After all, he wanted to show it to me. He was quite far away at the time, and I have no idea what might be so special about it. Now, I'd like to see it up close."

The parents, noticeably squirming, said they already had made their son reenact his exposure for them, but in the privacy of their family room, of course. They believed they had taught him a lesson.

"That's fine," Grandma said, "but now it's my turn. I'd like to see what's so special about it. After all, I couldn't see very well with all that water in my eyes." More squirming. But just when the nervous parents and teenage son were about to have seizures, Grandma smiled sweetly and said that she'd settle for the apology.

She got it quickly and honestly, and one young flasher hurried away from the dock where it all began. To Grandma's story, I can add only one thing: Hooray for Grandma.

12

Thumbnail Sketches

W hile assembling material for this book, I considered some 240 of 3,500 columns. All of them couldn't be included, but the more whittling down I did, the more difficult the task became. Finally, it seemed that the only way to include so many people who deserved a mention was to write summary capsules of some of the columns on people who made a difference. These folks really need to be in any book summing up twenty-five years of my writing for the Macon Telegraph. I hope you find these stories entertaining and inspiring.

Grady Sumner . . . is the granddaddy of a

town. He started repairing his own bike in the 1920s in Wrights-ville. His friends noticed how well Grady's bike was maintained, and they asked for his help. Since then, this gentle man, who made a living as a postal worker, has repaired bikes for three more generations—his daughter, Shelby, and her friends, his three grandchildren and their friends, and now his nine great-grandchildren and just about any other youngster who knocks on his door.

Those who could afford to pay helped him buy more parts. Those who could not afford to pay were never pressed. Because of his kindness, the youngsters of Wrightsville have been influenced in the best kind of way by Grady Sumner.

In 1990, Grady took me back to his childhood home just south of Wrightsville. He told me how ten Sumner kids used to sit around a fireplace in a tin-roofed house, share stories and stay warm through cold winter nights. And there was something good and right and wholesome about growing up that way.

And Grady did something that day I will not soon forget. He picked a few wild flowers near his homeplace. And he paused to smell them. Too few of us do that these days.

Nyesha Knight . . . revealed more courage at age

eleven than most of us ever have to muster. A brilliant student, a gifted athlete and a leader among the students at Jones Elementary School, she learned in 1995 that she needed a new heart. The one with which she was born suddenly dropped to an operating capacity of just thirteen percent—worse than the hearts of some older people after a heart attack. She rallied a school and a community to her cause. Some fellow students turned in their entire piggy banks to help out. Nyesha underwent a heart transplant in early 1996 and returned to class within a couple of months. She is doing well, and she continues to inspire everyone who knows her.

Iona Hutto . . . raised a family of achievers. In fact,

the influence of one parent seldom reaches into so many aspects of a school, but Mrs. Hutto, a widow, could claim three teachers at Houston County High School and a grandchild in every grade in the spring of 1996. And all of them were achievers.

Mrs. Hutto's children—Linda Harridge, Ronny Hutto and Cliff Hutto—had a combined seventy-three years of teaching experience at that point. Her grandchildren in high school at the time included: Chance Harridge, quarterback on the ninth-grade football team and a member of the varsity baseball team; sophomore Erin Hutto, a pitcher on the school state championship softball team and a rising basketball star; senior Ryan Hutto, president of the Future Farmers of America chapter at the school; and junior David Harridge, a member of the school's outstanding marching band. At one time, not only did all three of Mrs. Hutto's children teach, all three of their spouses were teachers, too.

Carl Peaster . . . has influenced as many lives as

anyone I know. As a coach at Macon County High School, Coach Peaster's basketball teams compiled an amazing record of 447 wins and just ninety-eight losses. Two winning streaks exceeded sixty games, and his teams won thirty-seven titles. But more than winning basketball games, Coach Peaster guided thousands of young lives in the right direction. His influence will not soon dissipate. And that's why the highway that runs past the school was named for him in the spring of 1996.

Chaplain Jack E. Brown . . . often

repaired lives above and beyond the call of duty at the Carl Vinson Veteran's Administration Medical Center in Dublin. I'll give you an example. In 1996, he drew three brothers together for the first time in sixty-eight years after he heard Edward Godbout's story. Seven Godbout children, he was told, went into a Vermont children's home after their father was killed in 1927, and all eventually wound up in foster care. They would scatter through three states. Edward married a South Carolina native and moved to Charleston after World War II, and he was a patient at the Dublin hospital when Chaplain Brown heard the story about the lengthy separation of siblings.

But the name was unusual, and, tracing backward by telephone and letter, Chaplain Brown located two sisters, Helen Gokey in Montana and Alma Casty in California, and two brothers, Al Godbout in Hawaii and Donald Godbout in New York. Chaplain Brown invited all of them to Dublin. The sisters were not physically able to make a trip, but the brothers came. They were reunited at the hospital in September of 1996.

Larry Benton . . . is one of Macon's good guys, a

hard-working fund raiser for organizations like the Jaycees, Riverside Optimist Club, the Boys Club of Macon and Tattnall Square Baptist Church. But his most memorable effort helped make the Veterans Memorial in front of the Macon Coliseum a reality. Two organizations were able to raise just $10,000 in eight years. Some $60,000 was needed to erect the memorial.

Larry Benton tackled the job and got the job done, and for decades to come, people will be admiring the marble monument containing the names of 484 men and women from Bibb and seven surrounding counties who died in the service of this country. There should be some permanent record of who ramrodded that project, and I hope Larry Benton will be remembered each time someone reads this book.

Melanie Venable . . . earned a spot in this

book because of her commitment as a single parent. Melanie's daughter, Kristina, was diagnosed with cystic fibrosis, and the young mom, a Macon police officer, made Kristina's survival Priority One from Day One. Melanie read everything she could find about the disease, and one article said swimming was just the kind of exercise that would keep a young body strong. So Kristina became a swimmer. A very good swimmer. She could go 25 yards underwater without breathing. In fact, when she was 7, she was competing against older children and winning. Kristina told me she wanted to swim in the Olympics some day. If she does, her mom ought to get a gold medal.

Bill Thompson . . . is tougher than old shoe

leather and as independent as anyone I've ever known. Bill was stricken by polio at age thirteen, just two years before Jonas Salk's vaccine began eradicating the disease in the mid-1950s. Even though he wound up with a brace on one leg and a crutch in his hand, this guy never leaned on the system to support him, never drew disability, never applied for Medicare. He simply got a good education and went to work.

In 1965, he took a government job and one of his assigned tasks was to redesign the camouflage patterns on aircraft and come up with new designs. He drew both the green patterns favored in the Vietnam War as well as the tan and brown patterns used during the Persian Gulf War.

Since Bill lives in Centerville, he sometimes glimpses military airplanes taking off and landing at Robins Air Force Base that bear his work. And I'm sure his chest surely swells a little with pride. And that's as it should be.

As this book goes to press, Bill is as independent as ever. He retired from civil service in 1990, but he still works several days a week at area antique malls.

S. L. and Ann Hilliard . . . certainly

deserve recognition, even though both passed on in the early 1970s. Their influence lives on in their eight children. The Hilliards of Rhine believed in family unity, and that meant husband and wife should be committed to each other. They practiced what they peached and they were married sixty years. Only death could make them part. Their children took note. Each of them chose a mate for a lifetime.

In 1993, four of their sons—Ray, June, Tal and V.C.—had each been married for at least fifty years. Two other children—Nell Hilliard Williams of Rhine and Roy Hilliard of Abbeville—had only one spouse each although they had not reached the fifty-year mark.

Even as grandchildren got married and had families, the Hilliards were seldom smitten by the divorce bug. S. L. and Ann Hilliard indeed set a good example for future generations.

Cogswell Cromwell . . . deserves a mention

in this book and a star in his crown because he volunteers his services—and tacks on a sense of humor for good measure.

Cogsy, as he is affectionately known, was one of the first to volunteer for the first Over-75 Birthday Party that was held for sixteen years at the Macon Coliseum. He was a kindly gentleman who, with the help of younger volunteers, loaded and unloaded physically handicapped guests. (Without repeat volunteers like Cogsy and Annie and Sammy Dame, we could not have afforded to hold the party.)

In 1991, Cogsy, then age eighty-three, called me and said he couldn't work that year. Said he was going blind. As my heart sank, he added, "But that isn't all bad. You see, I know a lot of ugly people!"

Any sympathetic words that were about to come out of my mouth were lost in laughter at my friend's sense of humor. And I told him, "You don't have to see, you old war horse. Just get on down here and boss these young'uns around." He did.

Violet Moore . . . became something of a legend

in the writing field. Although she was a small-town librarian (in Montezuma), Miss Violet was known far and near for her articles in the *Macon Telegraph*. But what endeared her to so many was her sense of humor. Folks were genuinely surprised to find out that this learned lady had never attended college.

"You mean you've *never* been to college?" a wide-eyed woman asked.

"Oh, now that you put it that way. . . . Why yes, I've been to college. Many times. To lecture."

What endeared her to me was that she knew *everyone* and she put me to work on stories in Montezuma and surrounding communities that she didn't have time to write. She sent me on so many good stories that people in other communities suspected I *lived* in Macon County. Georgia lost a great writer and I lost a wonderful friend when she passed on in 1992.

John Joshua Beasley . . . is included in this

book simply because he makes my daddy look not quite so prolific. You see, Mr. Beasley fathered *forty children*! My daddy fathered just eighteen. I found out about Mr. Beasley because one of his grand-daughters, Joan Boone of Warner Robins, wanted me to publicize a family reunion. Mr. Beasley had been dead for years when she contacted me in 1991. She said her cousins numbered "in the hundreds," including dozens that she'd never seen.

Mr. Beasley's children were born between 1877 and 1928, and one of them, Carlton, the fortieth child, was among more than 300 who gathered for the 1991 reunion. According to a 1929 story in the *Macon Telegraph*, Mr. Beasley was often whispered about. "Forty children!" exclaimed one woman. "Congress ought to do something for him."

Another woman huffed and said, "With forty children, Congress ought to do something *to* him!" Someone surely said the same thing about my daddy.

Betty and Felman Paster Jr. . . .

believe that the key to getting a good education is simply being there. That becomes obvious when I tell you about their children.

All six of the Pasters' offspring—Terrance, Keith, Radis, Prelvis, Pretandra and Curtis—earned perfect attendance certificates in Macon County schools for twelve years. That's right. Six children times twelve years times 180 school days per school term equals 12,960 days without a single absence.

Betty Paster said she would accept no excuses. The rule was simple: "Go to school or go to the doctor." She was indeed blessed with healthy children with good intentions.

Jack Elliott . . . preserved a part of our heritage in

old telephones. Jack worked for Southern Bell for thirty-five years, and when he retired in 1978, he didn't just walk away and forget the past. He filled his home in south Bibb County with one of the most extensive collections of telephones owned by any individual any-where. But Jack wanted to preserve more than just the telephone equipment he could put in his home. For instance, what about that big switchboard the folks at Robins Air Force Base were about to throw out? And what about . . .

Well, Jack got himself appointed as curator of the archives at Bell headquarters in Macon and he put together a most impressive museum of telephones, switchboards and other communications equipment. And, hopefully, it will be seen and appreciated for many years to come.

Faye and Charles Reese . . . certainly

earned a place in this book in the field of academics, not because they are teachers, but because they are caring parents.

The Reeses encouraged their children to be good students, but they would never have dreamed that three of four would be valedictorians at Jones County High. All four might have earned that honor except for one thing. The two youngest Reese offspring, Kerri and Karla, are twins. And, as you might have surmised, when Kerri was declared valedictorian of the Class of 1991 with a 98.70 average, sister Karla was salutatorian with a 98.48 average.

Faye Reese offered this summation of her children's accomplishments: "We tried to influence them, but we didn't pressure them. I'm equally happy with the personality and character they've developed. I'd choose them for the kind of people they are before I'd choose them for the grades they've made."

Mildred Henderson . . . surely needs to be

a part of this book since she was my second mama, and, indeed a second mama to most of those who worked in the *Macon Telegraph* newsroom in the 1970s and 1980s.

But Mildred's influence—indeed, a very good influence—ranged far outside the newsroom. She was once the editor of the *Telegraph*'s "colored news pages" before the practice of segregated news was discontinued. Knowing the kind of person she was, I often wondered how she coped with the situation, and one day I asked her. She explained it this way: "You do the best you can with what you've got. And don't ever dwell on the past. Lord knows, we all ought to learn from what we've been through, but we shouldn't dwell on it."

I followed her advice, and I was a better person for having known Mildred. Hundreds of other people will tell you the same thing.

Kristy King ♦ ♦ ♦ is a champion of the physically

challenged. Kristy's is the classic story of a great mind trapped in a body that is racked by cerebral palsy. In spite of battling the malady every waking minute . . . in spite of having to move around Wilcox County High in a wheelchair . . . in spite of frequent physical therapy sessions . . . in spite of all that, Kristy finished in the top five percent of her class, edited the school's yearbook and became the *STAR* student of the Class of 1996 when she scored 1,310 on the SAT test. She constantly impressed her teachers, but she absolutely captivated her classmates. She became both their friend and their cause.

Kristy's teacher, Celia McGlamory, summed up Kristy's presence this way: "Ever since I met Kristy, I've been looking down at her, but, all the time, I was looking *up* to her. She's an inspiration to us all."

C.R. Ward ♦ ♦ ♦ clipped folks for more than seventy

years to become the dean of Macon barbers. Mr. Ward told me when he was celebrating his eighty-seventh birthday in 1991 that he'd been in the business for seventy-one years and claimed these distinctions:

- He'd cut the hair of four generations of his own family, from his brothers to his great-grandson.

- He once gave eighty-eight haircuts in a single day—at fifteen cents a head.

- He saw the pay for his services rise from a dime a cut to six dollars.

- He'd given well over 200,000 haircuts in seventy-one years.

He was still clipping hair at Pete's Barber Shop on his ninetieth birthday.

Ted Sauls . . . was a great coach and a true friend to

little people who wanted to play ball. Ted's daddy was a great ball player, but he died when Ted was just a baby. Ted tried very hard to live up to his father's athletic image. In 1955 and 1956, Ted was an all-state tackle on a Monticello football team that won back-to-back high school state championships.

After he married and little Saulses began arriving, he turned to baseball and coached two sons, Teddy and Scott, and a daughter, Susan, through youth leagues.

But he helped mold many lives. He was president of the Jaycees, president of the football booster's club, a Sunday School teacher, a deacon at Monticello Baptist Church. And his wife, Margie, added one more thing: "He was the best daddy in the world."

Cancer took Ted Sauls's life in 1985. He was just forty-seven. People who knew and respected Ted Sauls named the baseball field in Monticello for him.

Murray Joiner . . . has planted more crops than

anyone I met in twenty-five years of covering the outback of Georgia. He was a few months past his ninth birthday when his father left him in a Dooly County field with the hired hands and one of them issued a challenge, "Bet you can plow a row as straight as any of us. Why don't you try it?"

Young Murray did. And, when his father saw what his son had done, he said, "Well, go down that row and back again." That happened in 1920, and Murray says: "I've been comin' and goin' down those rows ever since."

That's seventy-five years of field work. Is it a record? Probably not. But it's the best I know about.

Lettie and Charles Johnson . . .

certainly deserve a place in this book because they are the finest examples of parenthood anywhere.

Charles, who became a civil servant after a career in the Air Force, and Lettie, a nurse, promised each of their five children they'd pay for four years of college for each. And they made good on that promise.

In return, the children—Cheryl, Lori, David, Mark, and Jeffrey—promised to work hard in school and pick their friends carefully. And they made good on that promise.

All five earned college degrees. In fact, they hold a combined *eight* college degrees. All three sons graduated at the Air Force Academy and are now officers flying off into the wild blue yonder. Both daughters hold master's degrees. One is a school teacher and the other a high-ranking civil servant.

It wouldn't surprise me to see someone named Johnson from Macon on the Joint Chiefs of Staff some day. And you can remember I said that.